SUSTAINABLE HAPPINESS IN AN UNSUSTAINABLE WORLD

HODA ELSOBKY

PASSIONPRENEUR®
PUBLISHING

SUSTAINABLE HAPPINESS IN AN UNSUSTAINABLE WORLD

The Power of Being You in a World that Strives to Distract You

HODA ELSOBKY
Author of *DARE TO BE HAPPY*

Sustainable Happiness in an Unsustainable World
Copyright © 2025 Hoda Elsobky
First published in 2025

Print: 978-1-76124-211-3
E-book: 978-1-76124-213-7
Hardback: 978-1-76124-212-0

All rights reserved. No part of this book may be reproduced, stored in a retrieval system, or transmitted by any means (electronic, mechanical, photocopying, recording, or otherwise) without written permission from the author.

Because of the dynamic nature of the Internet, any web addresses or links contained in this book may have changed since publication and may no longer be valid. The information in this book is based on the author's experiences and opinions. The views expressed in this book are solely those of the author and do not necessarily reflect the views of the publisher; the publisher hereby disclaims any responsibility for them.

The author of this book does not dispense any form of medical, legal, financial, or technical advice either directly or indirectly. The intent of the author is solely to provide information of a general nature to help you in your quest for personal development and growth. In the event you use any of the information in this book, the author and the publisher assume no responsibility for your actions. If any form of expert assistance is required, the services of a competent professional should be sought.

Publishing information
Publishing and design facilitated by Passionpreneur Publishing
A division of Passionpreneur Organization Pty Ltd
ABN: 48640637529

Melbourne, VIC | Australia
www.passionpreneurpublishing.com

To Sara,
You are still my best achievement ...

ACKNOWLEDGMENTS

Thanks to you. To all the readers of my books, articles, attendees of my seminars, and followers online. You pushed me beyond my boundaries. Through you I saw a whole new world. A world where dreams come true, where purity, honesty, compassion and understanding reign supreme. Through you, I found inspiration and motivation to spread my wings and soar, to embrace my true self, and to appreciate the beauty within. Thanks to each message I received—it touched my heart, made me believe in each word, and enlightened my path.

Today, I owe it to you. You are amazing.

TESTIMONIALS

'Hoda provides a transformative blueprint for achieving lasting happiness and success through self-discovery and purposeful action. A must-read for those seeking to align with their true selves in a chaotic world.'

—HUMAIRA NASSIM
MASTERMIND AWARD-WINNING
AUTHOR OF **REDISCOVER** (2023)

'In her book, Hoda went beyond theories to provide practical insights and valuable tools to elevate the quality of life and sustain a high level of contentment and happiness.'

—AMR REFAAT
EXECUTIVE CONSULTANT
FORMER IBM GENERAL MANAGER

'**Sustainable Happiness in an Unsustainable World** offers a powerful and inspiring message that encourages readers to liberate themselves from negative emotions and self-imposed constraints. The use of the metaphor 'break the glass' suggests shattering barriers that confine one's potential for happiness. Overall, this sustainable happiness book written by Hoda Elsobky sets a transformative and uplifting tone, inviting readers to embark on a journey towards self-discovery and lasting joy.'

—OMAR HUSSEIN SIRAJ
THE INTERNATIONAL LITERARY CREATIVITY PRIZE
AWARD-WINNING AUTHOR OF **IMMIGRATION TO THE VIRTUAL WORLD** (2015–2016)

'This book is perfect for anyone who wants to practice the art of achieving happiness through real, practical steps. In a world that is demanding and continuously changing, we must look deep inside ourselves to find true meaning. This book made it possible for me to reflect and better understand the true purpose of the journey.'

—HOSSAM SEIFELDIN
EXECUTIVE VP & CEO CAPGEMINI EGYPT
FORMER IBM EXECUTIVE

TESTIMONIALS

'In **Sustainable Happiness**, Hoda Elsobky offers a thoughtful collection of easy-to-implement tips to keep you grounded in a hectic world. Following her advice will help you chart a successful path through life by ensuring your mental energy works for you, not against you.'

— TIMOTHY ROBERTS
EDITOR, PASSIONPRENEUR PUBLISHING

'This book takes you on a journey. As you embark on this journey, happy doors keep on opening.'

—ROSE MOSTAFA
SENIOR REAL ESTATE CONSULTANT

TABLE OF CONTENTS

Foreword by Kiran Shah.. xv
Preface xvii

Chapter 1
THE PURSUIT OF HAPPINESS
AN INTRODUCTION 1

Chapter 2
A JOURNEY TOWARD REDEFINING HAPPINESS
INTRODUCING THE 7-STEP ULTIMATE
HAPPINESS FORMULA 17

Chapter 3
AWAKEN YOUR TRUE POWERS
IGNITE YOUR PASSION AND TRANSFORM YOUR LIFE........... 35

Chapter 4
THE *REAL* YOU
THE BENEFITS OF BEING TRUE TO YOURSELF.......................... 57

Chapter 5
THE POWER OF EMOTIONS
UNDERSTAND THE NATURE OF YOUR FEELINGS
AND THE MAGNITUDE OF YOUR SENTIMENTS 75

Chapter 6
THE POWER OF QUESTIONS
MASTERING THE ART OF INTERNAL AND EXTERNAL
COMMUNICATION TO TRANSFORM YOUR LIFE 95

Chapter 7
THE POWER OF FOCUS
HARNESSING YOUR MENTAL ENERGY FOR SUCCESS 115

Chapter 8
BEYOND PAIN
EMBRACE PAIN AND REACH NEW HEIGHTS 129

Chapter 9
DO THE WORK!
NOTHING WILL CHANGE UNLESS YOU DO 145

Chapter 10
THE LAST CHAPTER
REST, STAY IN PEACE, AND WATCH THE MAGIC HAPPEN 159

Suggestions for Further Reading.. 177
References 179
About the Author... 183

FOREWORD BY KIRAN SHAH

'For times when we are not feeling our best, Hoda's book **Sustainable Happiness** is the ultimate antidote. Broken into step-by-step processes, it reflects Hoda's growth, wisdom, and progress since her last book. Her previous book, **Dare to be Happy**, spoke about a holistic approach to happiness, whereas **Sustainable Happiness** is more a detailed blueprint on achieving long-term happiness.'

—KIRAN SHAH
AWARD-WINNING COACH AND
AUTHOR OF **PINK SHOES & JILBAAB— NOT YOUR AVERAGE HIJAB GUIDE** (2021)

PREFACE

If you are addicted to sorrow, it's time to break that glass of sadness. Free yourself from doubts, limitations, and hate. Love yourself deeply, unconditionally, and without reason. Love yourself for who you are. I don't want you to be happy today—I want you to be happy forever. It's time to choose a better life, and claim your own happiness!

CHAPTER 1
THE PURSUIT OF HAPPINESS

An Introduction

In my continuous, consistent, and persistent quest to achieve happiness, I discovered that happiness *is* reachable and attainable, but being happy *consistently* is what really matters—that's the difficult part. Armed with this knowledge, I came up with the notion of *sustainable happiness*. I want to have happiness no matter what—or at least maintain an above-minimum-threshold level of contentment in life under any and all circumstances.

In my previous book, *Dare To Be Happy*, I discussed how to be happy and *stay* happy. In this book, I revisit and reinforce the value of being totally, genuinely, and honestly happy. Allow me to share my narrative, which serves as a reminder for all of us to reflect on our values, our passions, and the meaning we seek in our lives.

Remember that finding happiness and satisfaction is a personal journey, and taking the time to reflect and explore different paths is okay. I have been looking for happiness through every stage of my life.

It all started when I was 19. I wasn't clear about my goals, didn't know what I truly wanted, and lacked any clues or answers to my frequent and persistent questions. And, of course, I lacked the life experience to help me better understand myself. All I knew was that I had an ambitious, curious mind and was always passionate about understanding, learning, and enjoying life. I had questions: What is life all about? Where does true happiness lie? What would make me constantly happy and satisfied?

As a young girl, I looked for answers through the lens dictated to us by society. In the beginning, they seemed satisfying. After graduating from school with the highest honors, I attended my ideal university, then got the graduate job of my dreams with a reputable company I highly respected. At around the same time, I married the man I loved in a ceremony I'd always planned for. Living in the beautiful home I'd always wished for, I couldn't have been happier.

The pattern continued as I chased dream after dream, gaining status, power, and material possessions. All my goals had a common denominator: the *Material World*.

Having spent time trapped in an endless loop of thoughts, I know that the mind is never satisfied. I have been bound to a three-dimensional world, chasing ambitions—one after the other. Yet in the end, the pursuit of happiness itself made me tired!

At a certain point, the matrix my life was based on began losing its credentials and the loop of thoughts started to break into vicious circles.

Had I accomplished a deep sense of fulfillment and contentment in life? The answer was a clear *no*! I had to take a step back, then question and reflect on my values and passions to figure out what truly mattered to me. My husband and I realized that our appetite for having more and more had led to us having less and less of what truly mattered.

Having a child became our next dream. As self-proclaimed experts in attaining our goals, we exerted all the required effort and energy, not to mention the monetary and emotional demands. We traveled the world seeking help and consultation. During this time, we endured year after year of trials, distress, and desperation—along with patience, resilience, and grit, I must say! We found out that it was almost impossible to attain this particular dream of ours. Doctors confirmed that the chances of it coming to fruition were only 2 percent; this was honestly heartbreaking!

In a world where anything seemed possible, I found out that some of the things one sincerely desired weren't within reach. My deepest desire for motherhood—mutual love and connection, my craving to love and be loved, and my profound need to share my experiences, success stories and 'aha' moments—had come crashing down due to circumstances beyond my control. This setback became a deep-rooted wound that perhaps only those who've been through this same journey can fully empathize with.

Years went by in a mix of desperation and dashed hopes. It felt surreal that I was winning in the material world, yet losing in the meaningful one. Throughout the ordeal, I endured years of fragility and intense emotions.

My puzzled mind began to question the state: Why couldn't we have a child when everything else we desired was accomplished relatively easily? How could we survive such a profound sense of deprivation? How could we achieve happiness with only tangible possessions and status? For these questions, I had no answers.

Through these struggles, I've irrevocably grown wiser and gained a deeper sense of understanding of what truly matters in life. I began asking smarter questions and as a result, received better answers.

How could I translate my life experience into a story that could serve another person? How could I leave a legacy? How could I help others find joy in what's available? How can I find long-standing, grounded meaning in life, or the deep-seated joy of the soul? How can I be content without necessarily having it all? I settled for the answers I received at these moments in time.

More than thirteen years passed by. My husband and I had no reason to be optimistic. The only things we had at that time were hope, patience, and faith—hope that our dream would materialize one day, patience with the battle, and faith in God's wisdom and ability to manifest miracles.

And guess what? Hope, patience, and faith proved worthwhile. The 'aha!' moment took place, the miracle happened, and finally, the dream came true.

What I want to bring to light is that the struggle is real, and the pain is valid. The desire to understand life and find the answers to all of our questions is a part of who we are, but most of us seem to seek answers outside of ourselves, by following society's norms and aiming for predetermined milestones. This approach might have brought happiness and fulfillment for a while, but lasting happiness often comes from within; finding true happiness and satisfaction is a personal journey. The journey taught me the importance of finding the right guidance by looking inward and listening to myself.

Now, I'd love to invite you to share your experiences by writing down your story on the blank page at the end of this chapter.

What were your struggles? What have you tried? What 'aha!' moments did you have along the way? Have you felt a deep sense of contentment in your life? How long did it last? Did you find real meaning in your life? What is your true calling and passion? Look within for clues and answers, but don't settle for any resolution that doesn't satisfy your authentic soul.

Remember that self-reflection allows us to align our actions and goals with our authentic selves, leading to a more fulfilling life.

MOVING FORWARD, LET'S DELVE INTO PURSUING SUSTAINABLE HAPPINESS

Contentment is the biggest fortune a person can possess in life. Through it, you can achieve much of what you aim for—calmness, tranquility, and serenity.

By sustainability, I mean something that's capable of continuing. For example, when we talk about sustainable agriculture, we're talking about its ability to be maintained steadily without exhausting natural resources or causing severe ecological damage. The same applies to sustainable development. (Don't get overwhelmed by the technical terms; it's the broad idea that counts!)

I want you to reach a stage where you can maintain stable levels of happiness and fulfillment. It might help to consider it in the same way as sustainable living, which refers to being supported financially to cover all your basic needs. By seeing happiness through the same lens, you'll be able to support its prevailing nature throughout life. So, look at it as a way to support your dreams, realize your passions, reach your flow state, upgrade your lifestyle, develop yourself, and simply dance with life! Yes, *do* dance with life, because this is the most important skill you'll acquire after reading this book.

Now, I'd like you to close your eyes and imagine: Where are you now? Where do you want to be? What do you want to do in life? Who's going to be with you? Just allow your thoughts to flow.

Now, I want you to believe that you're already there ... because you are. Trust me, when you say 'I believe,' you're already halfway (if not all the way) there.

In my previous book, I wrote that 'dreams do come true.' I still mean it, too. Flow with your dreams, because they're destined to become true. This book is about dreams, achievements, fulfillment, hope, and love.

This book is about *you*.

I believe that with hope and love, you can conquer the world and make all your dreams come true.

AS HUMANS, WE'RE ENTITLED TO HAVE HOPE

Hope is the essence of life. Without hope, there is no life. I mean this. One of the strongest tools I've used in all of life's difficult moments is a weapon called *hope*. It's a feeling that what's desired can—and will—be realized sooner or later, no matter what. I always had a feeling that things would turn out for the best. I lived for a particular moment of this feeling: *the hope of winning*. This gave life a sense of adventure and curiosity, along with some fun and playfulness.

I always believe and trust, looking into the future with hope, ambition, and reasonable confidence. If you can, refer to my book *Dare to Be Happy*, and turn to Chapter 6, 'The Golden

Word', you'll find all you need to know about hope and its unwavering importance in improving people's quality of life and helping them make their dreams come true.

Next, I want to show you Figure 1.1, which depicts the foundation of all aspirations, expectancy, and longing. This handmade illustration dates back more than a century. I've seen it hanging on my grandmother's bedroom wall for many years, admiring it without quite understanding why. After a couple of decades, I came to understand what it meant—and why it had been passed down in our family from one generation to another.

The picture simply portrays hope in its purest and most unconstrained form. It depicts everything someone needs to know about life. It's summarized in one sentence: *Without hope, there is no life!*

This masterpiece is painted with earthy colors on pure silk. The beauty of the model and the simplicity of her dress enhance its style and allure. The model is a middle-aged lady of average size and build, illustrating the concept of moderation. The flowers surrounding her bare feet, the tree branches encircling her head, her long dark hair, her beautiful passionate and well-engraved features. All engender a sense of calmness, grace, and tranquility.

The woman raises her hands toward the sky, praying in a harmonious and refined manner. There's one word at the bottom, written in Arabic: 'Al-Amal,' or *hope*.

FIGURE 1.1: HOPE.

Look around, there are many people who suffer, yet they survive through the hardship. We shouldn't ignore the role of hope in cancer patients, psychotherapy, counseling, or even education—in every single domain of life, in fact. Hope is the essence of life, and if anything should be associated with humans other than the brain, I'd say it should be hope. All religions prompt us to be optimistic. What about all these new sciences, such as positive psychology, the science of happiness, and so on? All of them accentuate the importance of optimism. In the meantime, they motivate us to be encouraging to each other, cheerful, confident, bright, and happy.

Hope itself has the power to alleviate any situation and smooth the flow of life as we encounter obstacles, approach issues at work, or aim to achieve targets in our personal lives. The list goes on. As you might have noticed, I'm stressing the value of hope, as it's a major part of solving any problem at its roots. At this point, I encourage you to cultivate a sense of hope in how you think, feel, and solve your most strenuous and painful problems.

Promise me you'll start your day with hope and read this book with optimism, cheerfulness, and happiness. There's always a bright side, so begin seeing its colorfulness and radiance. Mute all internal and external disturbances and stay quietly and peacefully focused. I bet you'll think of millions of reasons to be grateful. Staying silent for a while will help you reclaim your power and rediscover your values, while identifying your purpose and mission.

Have you ever wondered why so many seemingly happy, successful billionaires and famous people—especially media personalities—end up dying by suicide, even though you thought they were leading the best possible lives? One example is Robin Williams, the beloved comedian and actor, who died on August 11, 2014. It was later disclosed that he'd been struggling with severe depression and anxiety, as well as the early stages of Parkinson's disease, which likely contributed to his decision to take his own life. Williams's tragic death shed light on the importance of mental health awareness and seeking help for those struggling with similar issues.

Returning to the disconnection between being famous and being happy, the mournful biography of Robin Williams reveals that we, as humans, tend to look at distinguished and successful people superficially. We view them the wrong way, from the wrong perspective. We gaze at a three-dimensionally constructed world, not at the level of their authentic selves.

Our natural state is peace, joy, and contentment. Anything that takes us away from our inner peace is an external material or tangible stimulant. Look inside and feel a deeper presence. Let the flow ignite within you; let life flow naturally, easily and unconditionally within, without expecting, judging, questioning, intervening or eventually blocking the flow of life within. I experienced the most glorious moments of success—no, they weren't even moments of success or breakthroughs … they were miracles—all while I was completely surrendering to the flow of life and God's will, and when I had no judgment whatsoever.

This book is a new level of understanding.

Happiness. Again and again.

WHAT IS HAPPINESS?

During these four years, specifically after publishing my first book, I earned a professional doctorate in coaching, a certificate of achievement in 'The Science of Happiness,' and more than five global awards. I was listed among the 500 Global Thought Leaders for two consecutive years by the Brainz Selection Committee (see Figure 1.2), as well as being invited to more than 17 interviews on the most prominent TV channels.

FIGURE 1.2: LISTED AMONG THE BRAINZ 500 GLOBAL THOUGHT LEADERS.

FIGURE 1.3. BRAINZ CREA GLOBAL AWARDS 2021.

My time as a public figure included speaking at many distinguished international universities and schools, as well as delivering a range of keynote speeches for multinational companies and government entities.

Aside from all the professional certificates and academic achievements, I've been a practitioner myself. Experience has taught me that *happiness comes from within*, and that we occasionally need discomfort to balance and give meaning to *happiness*. Negative emotions aren't bad, but how they're handled is key. You can express your feelings either positively or the opposite. Emotions are natural to human beings; it's how they're interpreted, felt, and processed that matters.

Emotions are a rich, yet complex, aspect of human life. Happiness, sadness, fear, anger, anxiety, boredom, jealousy, envy ... they all serve to guide, direct and motivate us to take action. Sometimes, they even *protect* us. Throughout this book, you'll learn to connect with and understand your emotions. Sometimes, even the most painful emotions can make you or break you.

As an in-depth researcher in the world of happiness, I picked up all the new and old books and scriptures I could find. I realized that every author has added a piece to the puzzle, and every thought leader interprets the messages to the best of their ability, as per their understanding and circumstances. I took several paths and embraced many disciplines and approaches. I started learning about the energetics of humanity, the quantum leaps, the laws of the universe, manifestation, and the laws of attraction. I read about Sufis.

An Empirical Examination

I received permission from S.H.—the CEO of a reputable telecommunications company—to write about how he succeeded in achieving a happy and enjoyable life as a result of our work together. Despite S.H.'s obvious success at work, he mentioned that he wasn't enjoying his life. He didn't have time for his wellbeing, socializing, taking breaks, pursuing his passions, or even spending quality time with his family. As a happiness coach, I could comprehend his emptiness and agony. Achieving success without authenticity holds no value. In other words, winning without being soulful is akin to gaining empty victories.

S.H. and I started working together in three dimensions: His health, his time (how he could get the most out of it), and his passions. S.H. was lucky enough to discover within himself a deeper understanding that he'd never sensed before. From here, he went ahead steadily with his life: He had his quarterly medical checkups done consistently, and recorded his sleep, eating, and exercise patterns until everything was on the right track and under control. He then started to fill his time with essential and enjoyable experiences. Later on, he rediscovered himself, his passions, and his talents. Needless to say, finding and loving himself led to him becoming able to savor every moment of success, while flowing with and learning to dance with life at its best.

I realized that everything you seek is already within you, and everything you look for is already looking for you.

The real work is within, not outside.

My book helps successful leaders who are struggling to lead enjoyable lives via a structured system that can easily be applied so they *can* have it all and win effortlessly on personal and work levels. Yet it also helps women in their 40s and 50s who struggle with the emptiness of the soul, feel busy doing nothing, and haven't yet been lucky enough to discover their talents. Through a systematic approach, I help them grab hold of their truths, so they can fulfill their inner needs and become unstoppable at manifesting their dreams.

Throughout my group's training and one-on-one coaching, I have a proven record of helping CEOs in the workplace, and women on both professional and personal levels, achieve *soulful success* and lead enjoyable lives.

CHAPTER 2

A JOURNEY TOWARD REDEFINING HAPPINESS

Introducing the 7-Step
Ultimate Happiness Formula

*'SUCCESS IS NOT THE KEY TO HAPPINESS.
HAPPINESS IS THE KEY TO SUCCESS.
IF YOU LOVE WHAT YOU ARE DOING,
YOU WILL BE SUCCESSFUL.'*

— ALBERT SCHWEITZER

Did you know that global happiness levels have remained relatively stagnant despite significant economic growth in recent decades? In fact, as the *World Happiness Report* reveals, there has been minimal increase in average happiness scores in recent years despite the considerable growth in material wealth. This suggests that conventional notions of success aren't enough to sustain long-term happiness.

From this point onwards, I resolved to redefine happiness as an *interior* state, which prioritizes fulfillment and passion over material achievements. This chapter introduces you to a range of techniques for embracing a more fulfilling life experience, simply by opening yourself up to new possibilities. The real work is within!

By adjusting your thoughts, self-limiting beliefs, the questions you ask yourself, the words you say to yourself, and your focus, you can create a whole new world for yourself.

In these pages, you'll learn a proven framework that unlocks your path to sustainable contentment, fulfillment, and achievement.

To help you achieve this, I'm pleased to introduce you to the 7-Step Ultimate Happiness Formula. This comprehensive framework helps you deeply connect with your inner self, overcoming emotional pain and disposing of limiting beliefs. With this program, you'll be empowered to live your most authentic and fulfilling life.

INTRODUCING THE 7-STEP ULTIMATE HAPPINESS FORMULA

I've broken down the Ultimate Happiness Formula into seven steps to help you follow the framework. Integrated throughout the book, these steps are easy to incorporate into your daily routine, creating a strong foundation for happiness.

Like anything else in life, fulfillment involves changing your habits. Habits can make you or break you; your success depends upon them. Whatever you're aiming for, choosing the right habits keeps you focused on it. If you want the body of your dreams, move toward that goal by acquiring good habits (going to the gym, eating the right food, seeing a nutritionist, and so on). Meanwhile, you'll also have to eliminate bad habits (including not getting enough sleep, emotional eating, and long hours of couch-sitting). It's not rocket science, right? By taking simple steps, you can reach big goals. The same goes for anything you want in life. Start by focusing on exactly what you want, then acquire the habits that will get you there.

To boost your own development, always start with small steps. This technique's known as *Kaizen*, the Japanese approach of taking small steps to achieve big goals. Originally designed for business, *Kaizen* focuses on continuous positive improvements. By breaking big goals into smaller, more manageable tasks, you'll be able to take small but consistent steps toward your objectives. In the process, you'll make steady progress, maintain momentum, stay motivated, and build habits for long-term success.

Here's my 7-Step Ultimate Happiness Formula, which I'll explore in more detail later:

1. Find your purpose.

Ask yourself: *What's my purpose in life?* If you can't find one, you're in serious trouble. Acting as the compass of your life, a purpose is the reason you wake up every day. It guides you to your destination, illuminating each day and driving your actions. It gives you energy, enthusiasm, and the power to navigate through life's ups and downs. A purpose can be anything that's worth pursuing—raising your children, for example. To achieve this major goal, you'll have to successfully pursue many smaller ones. These include going to work, making money, being a good role model, cultivating positive traits, shaping your children's personalities, spending time with them, protecting them, and simply watching them grow. Combined, these small goals add up to a purpose that's far more rewarding than any material achievement. Achieving this wider goal, though, may motivate you to pursue monetary attainment and success.

When identifying your purpose, I urge you to stay away from materialistic goals. Instead, identify a *real* goal more aligned with life's human side. By doing this, you'll build a sustainable sense of contentment with your life.

2. Tune in to the 'true you'.

The biggest mistake we all make is to disconnect from our authentic self. In other words, we disconnect from our souls, trying to step into others' shoes or follow rules dictated by society, colleagues, family, and friends about who we 'should be'. This endless chasing of happiness down blind alleys distances us from our essence, taking us far away from what we genuinely love.

> 'WHEN PASSION CAN'T FIND A WAY
> TO BE EXPRESSED, UNHAPPINESS AND
> IMBALANCES SURFACE.'
>
> — COACH URMILA RAO

Living your passion opens the path to purpose. 'When I root for my passion, I discover more of myself and connect more to my power,' Coach Urmila—author of *Meditative Musings* and former 'Meditate with Urmila' columnist with the tabloid edition of *Gulf News*—once said passionately. As for me, I wasn't truly attuned to my authenticity until I discovered my passion for writing at age 40. Fortunately, once people learn how to respond to their true self, they become unstoppable. How can anybody stop you from doing what you're meant to do on this earth? You're supposed to fulfill your passion—and I bet the only person who's stopping you is *you*.

If you're seeking energy every day of your life, I'd like to tell you about the secret articulated in Moustafa Hamwi's book *Live Passionately–The Blueprint to Design a Life Truly Worth Living*. As Moustafa says, 'Your passion = your energy, so if you want a return on energy, seek your passion.'

3. Understand your emotional state.

> 'CHANGE YOUR STATE, AND YOU CHANGE YOUR LIFE.'
>
> — TONY ROBBINS

You can change your physiology by changing your breathing. You can change your focus by deciding what to focus on. If your habit is to focus on the bad, there's no reason ever to receive good things. Instead, I *urge* you to start focusing on the good. If you want to achieve anything, set yourself in the right state. To write this book, I needed to be in a state of excitement and creativity—so I changed my emotional state (otherwise you wouldn't be reading it 😊). Do you know how to make yourself feel good? Using his coaching wisdom, Tony Robbins suggested listing at least 15 ways to instantly make yourself feel good. Inspired by his advice, I wrote a list to remind myself of what I love doing so I could change my state instantly. I like jogging, dancing, listening to romantic songs, reading on numerous topics, writing (of course), having coffee with friends, and playing with my daughter. I quickly reached 25 instant feel-good things that I like doing. Write your own list, updating it from time to time until you've reached 100 feel-good items. Then, use it to change your state—and your life—whenever you need to.

Don't underestimate the power of your emotions, because they shape your present and future in ways far beyond your comprehension. Emotions are a double-edged sword: They have the power to uplift you just as much as they have the power to bring you down. They can bring you good health, success, fulfilling relationships, happiness, and a high quality of life, while the contrary holds true as well.

4. Accept the power of questions and words.

The power of questions doesn't solely lie in the answers they generate, but also in their ability to unlock new perspectives, challenge assumptions, and lead us on a path of discovery. Questions are a very powerful tool. Ask the right question, and you'll get the right answer; ask smart questions, and you'll change the direction of your life. At many points, intelligent questions have changed my own life's trajectory. Whenever someone hurt or wronged me, I never asked myself how I could get revenge. Instead, I asked myself how I could turn the whole situation around. All of a sudden, I discovered hundreds of unexplored horizons and new possibilities. Our ability to change how we feel about something is immense: We can change our emotional intensity, examine a problem with a fresh perspective, and minimize the size of a problem. This is what I call *the art of leading your life*.

As Indira Gandhi once said, 'The power to question is the basis of all human progress.'

George Bernard Shaw offered his own take on things: 'Some men see things as they are and say "Why?" I dream of things that never were, and say: "Why not?"'

In his book *Awaken the Giant Within*, Tony Robbins described the situation best when he said that the only difference between the people who seemed successful and those who weren't was that successful people asked better questions. As a result, they got better answers.

Nothing I say about the importance of questions will be able to express their real value. Think about it this way, though: If you have a curious mind and ask questions (and by that, I mean consistently high-quality questions), congratulations! You're *definitely* increasing the quality of your life. The same applies to children from an early age. If your toddler's always asking too many questions—smart questions—whatever you do, don't get impatient. Remember, this is a sign of a curious mind—one that's analyzing all available opportunities, constantly considering what's possible and what's not.

In the end, the quality of the questions we ask is directly reflected in the quality of our lives. At any point in time, the questions we ask ourselves can change our conception of who we are, what we're capable of, and what we're willing to do to realize our aspirations and goals.

In the world of self-actualization and fulfillment, questions open up new horizons, revealing assets and opportunities that were previously hidden to us. I asked a client one question: 'Do you like the life you're leading?' 'In fact, no, I don't,' she replied. Then I asked her my *real* question: 'Why don't you design the lifestyle you'd love to live?'

A year ago, the same woman visited me. She told me that she'd since left her nine-to-five office job. Now working remotely as a freelancer, she's become wealthy by following her dream. You and I have limitless potential at our disposal. At any point, you can resolve to ask yourself the right question. Didn't get the right answer? Don't worry—at least you've opened a wide array of new possibilities.

Another of my clients was producing advertisements for well-known companies. Her employer's management team gave her a preselected set of 'vision boards', which she had to use for every new ad she designed. She wasn't happy with the situation. When I asked her what she didn't like about them, she replied that they lacked creativity, failing to keep up with the rapidly evolving digital world. That was the *perfect* reason to create her own designs and show them to the management team, I responded. Shortly after she found the courage to do so, her company chose her designs for the new framework.

In other words, you have to know exactly what you want—and what's stopping you from getting it.

Questions are powerful tools, with the capacity to unlock your hidden powers by changing the way you think. In the following chapters, you'll learn how to ask the right questions at the right time (and get the answers you're seeking), as well as the different types of questions—including the difference between empowering and disempowering questions.

For now, let's move on to another powerful tool: the power of the word. Generation after generation has ignored (or at least underestimated) the dynamism of the word. Whoever said words come and go was wrong. Words just *stay*! A single word can make you … and another one can break you. One word can make you happy, while another can make you sad. A word can unlock your potential, while another can deeply hurt you.

Can you believe that a *single word* of encouragement and reassurance in your time of need can change your life? It's true, because a well-chosen word can boost your confidence and instantly lift your mood. It can also stimulate your optimism, refresh your faith, and help you do things you never thought possible. A word of encouragement can reward you, comfort you, rescue you, and lift you up. So, choose your words generously and thoughtfully!

I once experienced what I call the *empowering, if not life-changing, power of words.* Freshly graduated from university, I was striving to get through as many job interviews as possible. Finally, I secured a long-awaited interview for my dream job ... which involved meeting all the board members. Honestly, I didn't believe I'd ever be offered an opportunity there. Incredibly anxious, I asked my teacher if she thought I'd be accepted. 'Yes,' she answered quickly and confidently. Confused, I looked directly into her eyes. 'You were always an above-average A student,' she explained. These honest words from my beloved teacher instantly changed my state, transforming me into a positive, happy, and confident person. What more could I wish for?

And guess what? I was accepted!

I'm sure a similar incident has happened at least once to everyone reading these words. Words can encompass a wealth of good deeds, inspire us to act, revitalize our energy, and endow us with exhilarating strength. By contrast, poorly selected words can discourage us, dishearten us, weaken our resilience, repress our motivation, and dampen our enthusiasm.

The *Creativity Approach* is a technique of awakening, elevating, and exalting the senses to bring on a creative mood. I choose to call it this, as it relies solely on the power of the words we choose in our daily interactions.

In my workshops, I consistently include a section about the power of words to change people's situation and achieve desired outcomes by sharpening their energy. This includes specific terms for defining success, closing deals, motivating personnel, transforming feelings, and directing actions.

All these ideas are consolidated in the 'Power of Questions and Words' section of my 7-Step Ultimate Happiness Formula.

5. **Utilize the power of focus.**

> 'THE SUCCESSFUL WARRIOR IS THE AVERAGE PERSON WITH LASER-LIKE FOCUS.'
>
> —BRUCE LEE

Focus is one of the most important skills you'll learn throughout this book. No matter what we've been taught about success and achievements, I always single out focus as a crucial factor behind any triumph. By focusing on the goal you want to accomplish, you'll see the invisible, achieve the impossible, and turn your dreams into reality. Whatever you choose to zoom in on materializes in the real world.

In the late 1800s, the renowned inventor Thomas Edison was working on perfecting the electric lightbulb. He'd already experimented with countless materials for the filament, but each attempt failed. One day, after a particularly discouraging experiment that didn't yield the desired results, Edison's assistant expressed their frustration, questioning the practicality of further attempts. Edison, known for his unwavering focus and determination, replied with great conviction, 'I have not failed; I've just found 10,000 ways that won't work.' This simple statement exemplifies Edison's ability to maintain an intense focus on his goal despite repeated setbacks.

Eventually, after countless hours of dedicated work and focused experimentation, Edison successfully invented a long-lasting and commercially viable electric lightbulb. Equipped with unwavering focus, he revolutionized the world with his groundbreaking invention.

This anecdote highlights the power of focus, demonstrating how relentless dedication and concentration can lead to incredible achievements despite numerous obstacles.

Now, let's return to the 7-Step Ultimate Happiness Formula. This is Step 5, where you focus all your effort on realizing your dreams, accomplishing your passion, and reaching a high level of self-actualization and fulfillment. That's all it takes to be happy—sorry, to be *sustainably* happy. 😊

To help you stay focused, I produced the following illustration for the **7-Step Ultimate Happiness Formula:**

A JOURNEY TOWARD REDEFINING HAPPINESS

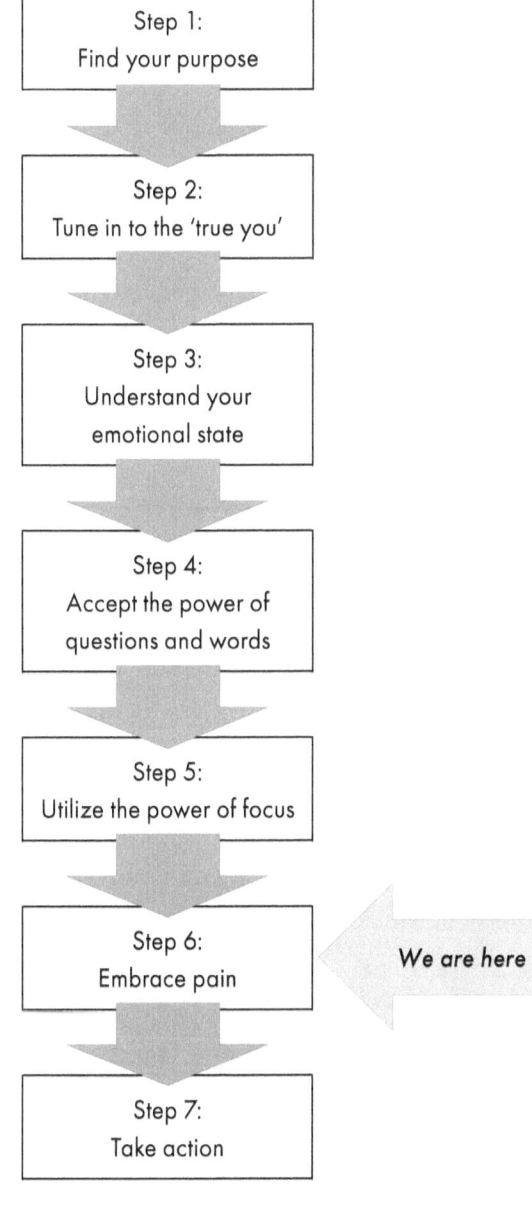

6. Embrace pain.

I've never seen a more powerful mechanism than pain, which can trigger swift yet sustainable change. The change following pain is momentum leading to a breakthrough that can offer life-changing opportunities.

Remember the prominent proverb that says, 'Opportunity knocks but once'? Opportunities are rare and should be seized when they arise, because they may not come again.

That's it. You can either grasp the opportunity when it presents itself and make the most of it … or let it slip through your fingers, to your perpetual regret. Choosing the second option triggers feelings of despair, missed potential, and unfulfilled dreams. It often leads to lingering questions about why you didn't take action at the time, or what could've been achieved if the opportunity was seized. I firmly believe that pain serves as the catalyst for meaningful change. When the discomfort of staying the same exceeds the discomfort of change, that's the pivotal moment when decisive action must be taken. In other words, once you reach a threshold where the pain of following the status quo is greater than or equal to the pain of change, that's when the bullet comes out of the pistol and hits the target—the change you have to make.

> **The pain of staying the same** ▶ or ▬ **The pain of change.**

I'm not here to pursue change for change's sake. To embrace change, though, you need to upgrade your life by reaching for the stars. Earlier, I mentioned that I want you to be happy—not only today, but forever. This is what I call sustainable happiness, which is the essence of my book *Sustainable Happiness in an Unsustainable World*.

7. Take action.

In the end, we only regret the things and the choices we didn't make. In the words of the Austrian-American management consultant, educator, and author Peter Drucker, 'The best way to predict the future is to create it.'

Producing results isn't as challenging as it might seem, but *preparing* to produce results is. The way you get yourself ready, put yourself in the mood to win, handle and manage your emotions, and control your behavior and actions is what makes a winner or a loser. It all starts in your mind, with the way you think!

Take athletes, for example—think of how they prepare to win through a combination of physical, mental, and strategic preparations. As winning begins with the mind, athletes usually concentrate on aspects such as focus, strength versus pain points, confidence, and fear of failure (we'll talk later about redefining failure). They'll also draw on a range of enhanced techniques, such as visualization, positive self-talk, clarity of purpose, and embracing a passion for winning. Athletes work with coaches, trainers, and mentors to develop effective tactics and approaches that offer a competitive advantage.

Similarly, you'll learn how to take steps toward the right goals while prioritizing your most cherished values. In the process, you'll discover how to identify your targets, eliminate distractions, and reach the point of convergence. (Consider it the magician's way, where life's never the same again.) Ironically, I don't believe in magic, but I *do* hold faith in miracles—and the idea that dreams are destined to come true.

Work through the 7-Step Ultimate Happiness Formula with me to find your true calling and experience a quantum leap in your life experience.

Finally, I believe that everything happening in your outer world is a direct reflection of your own behavior and what's happening within. (Of course, this does not apply to *force majeure* or circumstances beyond your control.) I invite you to embark on a captivating journey with me filled with knowledge, inspiration, and the joy of discovering a whole new world full of possibilities. Welcome, fellow wanderer, explorer, and fortune hunter. Let's begin ... and let the fun begin.

WHAT'S NEXT?

Throughout the following chapters, we'll delve deeper into each part of the 7-Step Ultimate Happiness Formula. There are seven stages, with each chapter bringing you closer to achieving your goals. Emphasizing the importance of each phase throughout this journey, we explore profound themes such as purpose and meaning, authenticity, emotions, the transformative power of questions and words, the importance of focus, embracing discomfort, and taking decisive actions. At the end, we'll move together into the final bonus chapter, which implores us to simply rest and watch our dreams materialize like magic.

Chapter 3

| FIND YOUR PURPOSE | ← *We are here* |

| TUNE IN TO THE 'TRUE YOU' |

| UNDERSTAND YOUR EMOTIONAL STATE |

| ACCEPT THE POWER OF QUESTIONS AND WORDS |

| UTILIZE THE POWER OF FOCUS |

| EMBRACE PAIN |

| TAKE ACTION |

CHAPTER 3
AWAKEN YOUR TRUE POWERS

Ignite Your Passion and Transform Your Life

Did you know that discovering your purpose is like finding the key that unlocks the door to a life filled with passion, fulfillment, and endless possibilities? Many people live and die without knowing what they truly want to do, what their goal is, what their passion is, and what strengths they possess. You can be a single step away from your true calling without knowing that taking this last step would lead to a whole new horizon—a time when life's never the same again, where you become limitless and unstoppable by tuning in to your true potential. Your success becomes unavoidable, and you shine brightly like a star. You simply release the giant within.

Do you remember a time when you felt lost or didn't know what you really wanted, who you authentically were, or what would make your soul happy? This chapter will enable you to discover who you really are, your purpose in life, your true passion, and your genuine strengths.

Are you ready to embark on a transformative journey toward discovering your life's purpose? Many yearn to begin this quest. How can you uncover the elusive answer to the fundamental question: *What's my purpose in life?* Let's start by highlighting the importance of having a sense of purpose and direction.

DOES HAVING A PURPOSE INCREASE LIFE EXPECTANCY?

A purpose in life is as important as breathing; as long as you live, you need one. Your life's purpose is like a compass that guides you through life. Purpose keeps you active, motivated, and excited each day of your life. Yet its importance extends far beyond this—it can directly affect your life expectancy.

- There's a correlation between depression and lacking a purpose in life. Social statistics have shown that people with a greater sense of purpose are less likely to be depressed; therefore, they're more likely to achieve their goals. Additionally, they're more likely to experience higher life satisfaction and overall happiness. A 2019 study published in *JAMA Psychiatry* analyzed data from nearly 7,000 adults over 50 and found that having a strong life purpose was associated with a lower risk of developing a major depressive disorder. Thus, we can conclude that having a purpose is a strong shield against major depression, especially in older age.
- Research in various fields such as psychology, health sciences, and sociology continues to shed light on the

fact that having a strong sense of purpose improves physical and mental health as well as enhancing overall quality of life. An example of a source study is J. Smith and A. Johnson's 2021 *Journal of Health* article, 'The Importance of Purpose in Life in Health and Healthcare Innovation', which provides further insights into the benefits of having a strong sense of purpose in enhancing overall wellbeing.

- People with a strong sense of purpose often have higher levels of motivation and determination, which can be significant factors in achieving success. When individuals have a clear direction and a purpose aligned with their values, they have the focus and drive to overcome obstacles and accomplish their goals.
- Having a strong sense of purpose can increase resilience. When faced with challenges, such individuals are more likely to view them as temporary obstacles than as insurmountable barriers. This mindset can help them bounce back quickly, learn from their experiences, and pursue their goals with renewed determination.
- Purpose-driven individuals tend to have a clearer vision for their lives, enabling them to make decisions aligned with their values and long-term objectives. This clarity often leads to more effective goal setting and planning, increased productivity, and better time management—all factors contributing to greater accomplishments in life.

Now that you've read the above, it's a good time to begin writing your life purpose on the blank page at the end of this chapter. As you're doing this, remember that your purpose isn't fixed. First, you need to determine a clear purpose to structure your goals around. Engage in self-exploration, continuously refining your goals until you've reached the core of what you long to achieve.

A purpose can change at many stages of life. So remember to maintain flexibility when writing down your purpose, as you'll return to this many times over the years. While writing down your true purpose, be ready to unlearn old purposes that no longer serve you. Meanwhile, strive to close the gap between who you are now and who you want to become. This requires driving your attention and focus to new heights, sharpening your motivation and energy.

How can you uncover and embrace your true purpose?

Or, to put it differently: *What is your purpose in life?*

What are your top 10 values? What are the top three values you can't live without? What would you still love doing, even if you had all the money you needed? And here's the billion-dollar question: What would you do for a living if you were given a check in your name for ten billion dollars? $10,000,000,000! Think it over again, then write down the first three answers that come to your mind. Now, think about the opposite: What would you want to do for a living if you had to work for free?

Your answer to these two seemingly contradictory questions should be the same!

Do you still doubt your true potential, passions, and credentials? Let's answer some tailored questions, which will bring you closer to uncovering your profound meanings, values, and passions. Take time to engage in self-discovery. Ask yourself: What do I enjoy doing? What brings me joy and fulfillment? What are my strengths and talents? What values are important to me?

Then, keep on answering: What triggers my interest? Which topics captivate and intrigue me? What things are easy for me, yet hard for others? What kind of books do I read? What TV shows do I like? What do I *really* love doing? What do I spend my money on willfully? Which activities cause me to lose track of time, and even to forget about food and drink? What topics energize and enthuse me? Which activities utterly absorb me? If I were to write a book, what would it be about?

It's always better to write down your answers, refer back to them, and update them occasionally. Now, if you're still not sure about your values and passions, let's explore further strategies:

- Explore your interests by engaging in a wide range of activities. Volunteer, join clubs and organizations, take up hobbies, or try a different career. This will help you

discover what resonates with you the most and ignites your passion.
- Seek feedback from others. Reach out to close friends, family, mentors, or trusted advisers, asking for their perspectives on your strengths and passions. Sometimes, others can offer valuable insights that we might overlook.
- Use assessment tools. Consider taking personality and aptitude assessments such as the Myers-Briggs Type Indicator (MBTI) through https://www.themyersbriggs.com/en-US/Products-and-Services/Myers-Briggs, a widely used assessment that categorizes individuals into 16 personality types based on preferences. Another test is the Big Five personality traits (IPIP) through https://ipip.ori.org/, which evaluates individuals across five personality dimensions: openness, conscientiousness, extraversion, agreeableness, and neuroticism. There's also the DISC assessment, a popular personality test based on the DISC theory of psychologist William Moulton Marston which assesses behavior and communication styles based on four personality traits: dominance, influence, steadiness, and conscientiousness. You can find it through the official website of Extended DISC (https://www.extendeddisc.org/). There are also aptitude tests and career assessment tests. The feedback generated by your results can provide insights into your personality traits and strengths, as well as revealing potential career paths aligned with your interests. Examples include StrengthsFinder, Holland CODE (RIASEC), the 'Strong Interest Inventory' at https://thepersonalitylab.org, and https://www.themyersbriggs.

com. These assessments can be valuable tools to gain self-awareness, understand your strengths and weaknesses, and explore career paths that align with your personality traits and interests.
- Try journaling and writing. Maintain a journal where you regularly write about your thoughts, feelings, goals, wishes, and plans. Write about what you want to achieve in the real world. This can be a powerful tool of inner understanding, helping uncover patterns and themes that symbolize your true calling.
- Seek inspiration. Read books, listen to podcasts, and watch documentaries or TED talks about personal development, purpose, and finding one's passion. Learning about others' journeys, lives, biographies, and experiences can help you gain insight and inspiration.
- Experiment and take action. Once you've formed ideas about your purpose and passion, act and experiment. Try out different paths or projects, even on a small scale. By taking action, you can gain more clarity, make adjustments, and refine your path along the way.

Ultimately, as you grow and evolve as an individual, trust the process, be patient with yourself, and stay open to new experiences and possibilities. With a clear vision of your life goals, passion, values, and strengths, you'll never be bored again. That's because you'll have a list of the things that ignite a fire in you, which you can refer to whenever you like. That's what I call *the art of never getting bored again!*

 Further reflections

Let's talk about boredom. Boredom itself isn't bad; in fact, many readings suggest that boredom ignites creativity. For instance, when someone is bored, they might look for outside-the-box solutions. This, in turn, can trigger a sense of creativity, artistic endeavors, and resourcefulness, thus paving the way to originating inventive works. For the context of this book, when we discuss boredom, we're particularly talking about boredom as a void, non-engagement, or just being 'unbusy'—or busy doing nothing!

Looking for more inspiration and profound insights to guide you? Read my article in the September 2020 edition of *Brainz Magazine*. Here's the link:

https://www.brainzmagazine.com/post/did-you-ever-dare-to-reinvent-yourself

Ask yourself:
Am I ready for my purpose to proclaim itself?

By now, you should understand more about your passion and values. You should know that you're destined to do something meaningful—something that can inspire your curiosity, creativity, attention, and focus, as well as repeatedly bringing excitement, drive, and motivation into your life. This is something to embrace as your standpoint, as well as to offer others. To do all of this, we must find meaning in life that's capable of evolving with us.

THE IDENTITY GAP

We must identify and close the gap between who we are and who we want to become. As discussed above, your purpose requires you to make progress by becoming a new version of yourself, thus fulfilling the need to become who you want to be and achieve the success you desire.

Many authors have addressed this perspective of the identity gap. For example, here's a resourceful quote by Marie Forleo, in her book *Everything is Figureoutable*: 'No matter what you are facing, you have what it takes to figure anything out and become the person you are meant to be.' Forleo stresses the importance of embracing a growth mindset (rather than a fixed one) to achieve your desired self by bridging this gap. Or, in Maya Angelou's words, 'Do the best you can until you know better. Then when you know better, do better.'

Closing the status gap

In terms of personal development, many psychologists and sociologists emphasize the importance of authenticity, self-awareness, and self-acceptance. The more someone works on meeting their needs and aspirations, the closer they are to closing the gap between their current self and their future wished-for self, and the closer they get to achieving happiness, fulfillment, and inner peace.

This can be more visible during college, where students strive to acquire the precise skills to secure their dream job or wished-for status. The more this gap is closed, the higher a person's wellbeing and life satisfaction, the more fulfilled they'll become, and the higher their probability of success. That's why reducing the status gap is essential for personal growth.

Closing the identity gap

Between these two versions of yourself—who you are and who you want to be—there's the journey of filling the gap. First, you need to become the person with that ideal level of success. The universe won't deliver something you're not a match for, so you have to *be* that version of yourself that's aligned with your desires. That's how you close the gap. For example, assume you want to become one of the best public speakers in your field of expertise. What you need to work on is:

- Increasing your knowledge in that area of expertise.
- Increasing your level of confidence and self-esteem.
- Creating impactful and useful content.
- Improving your communication and presentation skills.
- Learning the required technical skills to get your work done.

All these steps are necessary, but you must first shift your thoughts and beliefs to position your energy behind the success you want to see. To do this, you'll have to become more trusting in yourself and your work, confident, and committed to the end result while clearing any resistance (see Figure 3.1a and 3.1b).*

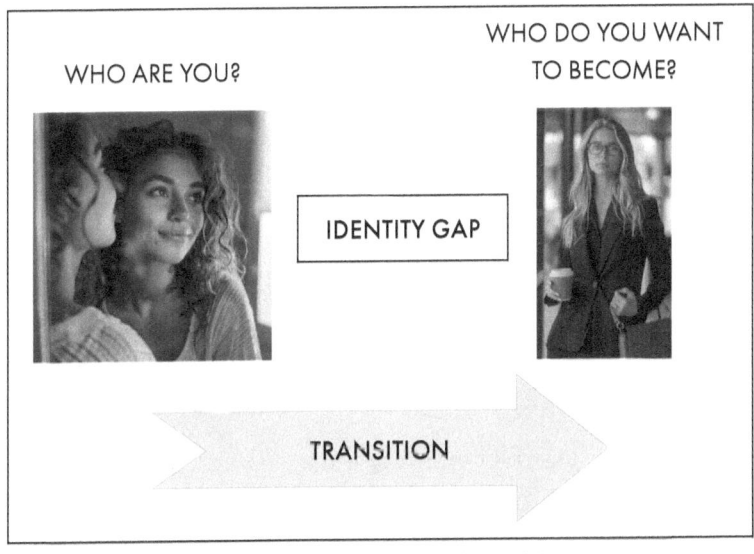

FIGURE 3.1A: CLOSING THE IDENTITY GAP.
*Photos are AI-generated

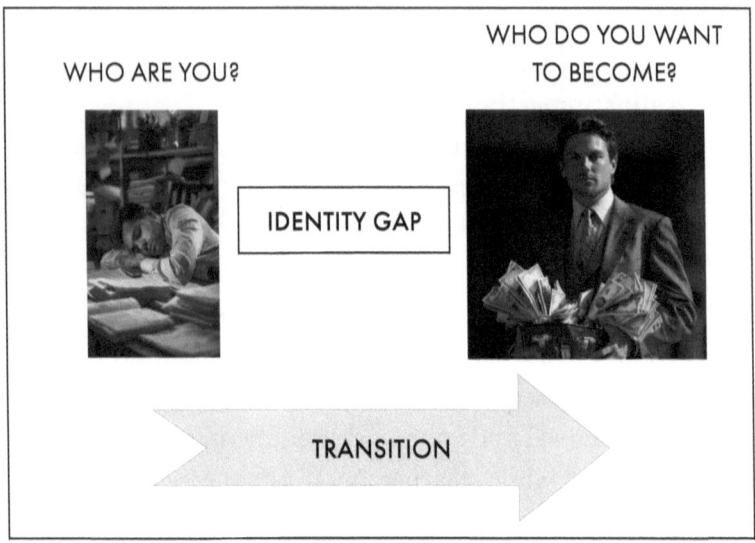

FIGURE 3.1B: CLOSING THE IDENTITY GAP.
Photos are AI-generated

Several social studies, notably in positive psychology, have shown that we experience the most happiness at the intersection between our authentic and desired selves. This gray area is where you reach harmony between *who you are* and *who you aspire to be*, achieving a series of goals aligning with your values and interests. At this point, we allow ourselves to become authors of our lives and directors of our fates, thus contributing to greater happiness and life satisfaction.

Once you've identified your big purpose and structured your goals around it, it becomes easy to locate the areas of growth you'll need to tackle to become the best version of yourself. Once your new goals are set, your daily experiences, routines, and habits will transmit you to your larger purpose. In other words, once purpose and identity are aligned with your values, happiness prevails (see Figure 3.2).

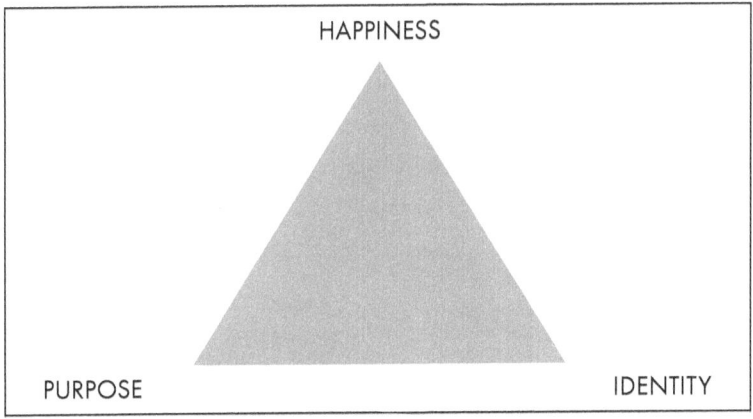

FIGURE 3.2: ACHIEVING NEW GOALS: THE HAPPINESS TRIANGLE.

Bonus Material

For more clarification on this topic, scan the above QR code or visit my Instagram page (elsobkyhoda) and go to the #MondayLive episode titled 'Who you are and who you are becoming.'

YOUR PURPOSE CAN EVOLVE THROUGHOUT THE DIFFERENT STAGES OF YOUR LIFE

Let me tell you the story of the Nigerian billionaire Olufemi Peter Otedola CON, born November 1962. A businessman and philanthropist, he's currently the Executive Chairman of Geregu Power Plc. This is a true story I heard once, and I like the positive impact it has on me each time I recall it.

This man found his true purpose in life. His goal started with making money and collecting precious things, then progressed to running a series of giant successful projects. Finally, he realized that his purpose in life wasn't fixed, but ever-evolving. He understood that his talents and passions could be harnessed to bring joy and meaning to his and others' lives. This man embraced the idea that his purpose could revolve around spreading love, kindness, and inspiration through his acts.

Now, allow me to retell this story from my own perspective. In my opinion, it's the story of one of the happiest men in the world. Do you know why? It's because he not only discovered his true purpose in life, but also embraced the ever-changing nature of existence. In other words, he discovered that his life had a greater meaning than he previously imagined.

Here's how the story goes. In an interview with Otedola, the host asked, 'What was the event that made you the happiest man on earth?'

Otedola explained that he'd passed through four stages in life before understanding the real meaning of happiness. First, he collected money through hard work, thinking true happiness could be found there. Next, he collected precious objects, thinking true happiness could be found *there* instead. When he discovered that this idea of happiness was only temporary in nature, he started running major projects. Otedola ultimately became the sole proprietor, managing 95 percent of the diesel through Africa. Even then, though, Otedola confessed, 'I didn't feel the happiness as I imagined it to be.'

Otedola's life permanently changed, he said, when 'a friend of mine asked me to buy 200 wheelchairs for needy handicapped boys. My friend insisted I go with him to deliver the chairs, and so I did. That day changed my life. I saw happiness in their eyes like I'd never seen it before. Kids were sitting on their chairs, running and playing as if they were on a trip and looking forward to the big prize. Before we got ready to leave, one boy stopped me and grabbed my hand, and I said, "Do you need anything, little boy?" He said, "No, I just want to remember your face well so that when I see you in heaven, I can thank you again."'

If I had to choose a name for this story, it would be 'The Pursuit of Purpose'.

In conclusion, fulfillment doesn't come from achieving a single goal, but instead from embracing the journey of self-discovery.

Below, I've summarized some objections that may arise at this point.

Q1: What if I can't find a purpose that ignites a spark in my life?

A1: Everyone in this world has something that lights them up. Some are lucky enough to find it when they're young, promptly kicking off their journey toward a purposeful life. These people, who are quick to discover themselves, usually reach career success early on.

They rapidly realize that what they love, what they're good at, what the world needs, and what they can be paid for doing are the same thing, simultaneously finding their passion, mission, vocation, and profession. Knowing what brings meaning and joy to every day of their lives, they unleash their *ikigai*—the Japanese secret to a long and happy life, according to Héctor Garcia and Francesc Miralles in their book *Ikigai*.

I encourage you to take the time for introspection, to think about past experiences that brought you joy and a sense of purpose. By exploring new interests, activities, or hobbies, you may also discover something that resonates with you and reignites your passion. Seek inspiration from people you admire or who have found their purpose. You can also seek support by contacting family, friends, a support group, or a life coach. Sometimes, discussing your thoughts and feelings with others can provide new insights. Finally, be patient with yourself and embrace uncertainty, as finding your purpose can be a journey filled with doubt. Remember, what may seem unclear now may become clearer in the future.

Q2: What if I don't have what it takes to fill in the identity gap between who I am now and who I want to become?

A2: You will, once you know who you really want to become, and you have enough clarity. You have to feel that you're already on the level of the person you want to become, and be able to convincingly embody that person. The universe won't deliver something you're not a match for. You need to shift your thoughts and beliefs first, then action will follow. It's not about the outcome, but instead about the energy behind the action. Your thoughts should focus on the excitement your desires manifest, not the frustration of lacking what you want. Only the power of thoughts can activate your desires. You must feel worthy of your desired success, aligning your energy, thoughts, and beliefs. From this point, you can seek to fill the gap. For example, you might need to earn a certification, learn a new skill, or lose weight. Beginning from a point of abundance and worthiness, you can start fulfilling your dreams. You have to *feel* able to change your reality and create a world that fulfills your needs. More in-depth explanations about thoughts, beliefs, focus, alignment, and creating vibrations that can activate your dreams unfold in the next chapters.

Q3: What if I had a sudden shift and my old purpose became irrelevant?

A3: It's common for individuals to alter their sense of purpose throughout life. Our priorities may shift as we grow and learn, making our previous purposes less relevant (or even obsolete). This is normal: Because we develop new purposes as we evolve, it's essential to shed former identities that no longer serve us. If your purpose has changed, it can be an opportunity for growth and self-development. Understanding your core values and passions can help you identify a *new* purpose that aligns with your current stage of life. As a result, you repeat the process of fulfilling your new purpose, adjusting your goals, and reaching a joyful stage of accomplishment.

CHAPTER TAKEAWAYS

In this chapter, we learned how to discover your purpose and uncover your potential by tapping into your talents to become the person you aspire to be. We know that purpose isn't fixed; it can change at each stage of life. Therefore, we should be flexible enough to adjust our life's purpose according to age, conditions, and circumstances. Renewing our major life goals, then, is imperative. If you discover that your main purpose is becoming irrelevant or obsolete, don't be afraid to let go and find your new one. The story of Femi Otedola, the Nigerian businessman, offers convincing proof that our purpose can evolve throughout the many stages of our lives. Finally, we understand how the dynamics of the triangle work: purpose, identity, and happiness. Whatever you do, always start with your strengths in mind.

To reach self-actualization and lead a more fulfilling and purposeful life, consider these actions.

Actions for readers

1. Clear your mind by decluttering anything unnecessary that's filling your head. Only then will you be in a position to receive new insights that can serve you in the journey to come.
2. Unlearn goals or purposes that no longer serve you. Many of your old dreams have now been invalidated, lost their spark, or proved wrong or unfulfilling. Some have already reached their expiry date. Don't be scared to unchain these dreams and goals. Set yourself new, more valid ones instead.
3. Get excited about establishing fresh objectives and receiving new experiences, which in turn can invigorate your mind, enrich your life, and awaken your senses towards growth, joy, and fulfillment!

WHAT'S NEXT?

Finally, when it comes to purpose, the process can take many years. This book will help you find comfort in distinguishing your purpose and recognizing your goals. Each chapter will add value to your cumulative adventure, leading to joy, determination, and decisiveness about your next dream goal. I suggest reading each chapter at your own pace, to reflect and absorb its knowledge. Remember to reward yourself after each one, watching closely as your personal growth unfolds. You've done well, so treat yourself to a moment of celebration. Your journey awaits.

The next chapter is a profound reflection on the importance of connecting and understanding yourself. By 'yourself', I mean your true self; in other words, your purest essence.

YOUR SPACE

Chapter 4

| FIND YOUR PURPOSE |

| TUNE IN TO THE 'TRUE YOU' | ← *We are here*

| UNDERSTAND YOUR EMOTIONAL STATE |

| ACCEPT THE POWER OF QUESTIONS AND WORDS |

| UTILIZE THE POWER OF FOCUS |

| EMBRACE PAIN |

| TAKE ACTION |

CHAPTER 4
THE *REAL* YOU

The Benefits of Being True to Yourself

Are you living in someone else's shoes, or embracing your true hues? Knowing how we navigate life paints a vivid portrait of who we truly are. Cherishing our own choices is crucial, because they tell a tale crafted just for you.

Have you ever wondered how much of what *should* be your own time is already defined by others? How many times have society's expectations silenced the true you?

What if you suddenly realized that all your self-beliefs were wrong? Have you ever wondered what it would be like to start over, free from past expectations? What if the key to unlocking your true potential lies in confronting your deepest fears and insecurities? What if discovering your true self meant letting go of everything you *thought* you knew?

This chapter explores the significance of tuning in to your authentic self. In a world that encourages conformity while masking our genuine personalities, it's essential to reclaim our true essence by living in alignment with who we truly are.

I've provided practical insights, exercises, and guidance to help you reconnect with your authentic self. You'll learn how to decipher the difference between societal conditioning and your soul's desires. Shedding your layers of inauthenticity will give you the confidence to express your true thoughts, feelings, and beliefs.

MIND CONNECTIONS

Do you remember a time when you sat with your thoughts, listened to that voice inside your head, eliminated all distractions, and connected with your essence? At this pinnacle, you touched base with your most creative desires, thought outside the box, and assimilated extraordinary mind connections that solved your most challenging problems in phenomenal ways.

I need you to feel the power of now in this moment, where you embrace who you truly are and what you want. Don't worry—you won't have to conform to any external expectations or stereotypes.

You just have to be you, act like you, talk like you, walk your walk, and dance to your own rhythm.

Simply by being yourself, you'll experience freedom and liberation. You'll cultivate acceptance and self-love. You'll recognize that you're worthy and valuable just as you are. You'll attract like-minded connections, as people are drawn to your authenticity.

Most of all, you'll tap into your unique strengths, talents, and passions, allowing you to fully express yourself and contribute to the world in more meaningful ways.

Last but not least, living in alignment with your true values brings about a deep sense of fulfillment. It can provide a roadmap for your life choices and actions, guiding you toward outcomes aligned with your deepest convictions.

To illustrate how aligning your values with your purpose can bring about deep fulfillment, let's consider the story of Hussein.

THE IMPORTANCE OF LIVING IN ACCORDANCE WITH YOUR ETHICS

Hussein had always been a dedicated environmentalist who was deeply passionate about protecting the planet and advocating for sustainable practices. However, in his early career, he found himself working for a corporation that prioritized profit over conservation. Despite being well-compensated, Hussein felt a growing sense of conflict within himself every day he went to work.

Increasingly disconnected from his values, Hussein decided to change. He quit his corporate job, seeking environmental advocacy opportunities in the non-profit sector. It was a challenging transition both financially and professionally, but Hussein knew he needed to align his work with his core beliefs.

As Hussein immersed himself in his new role, he experienced a profound shift in his sense of fulfillment and purpose. By dedicating his time and energy to a cause he deeply cared about, he felt a renewed passion that was missing from his previous job. Knowing his actions made a positive difference in the world helped him find joy and meaning in his work.

Hussein had learned firsthand the transformative power of living in alignment with his values. He discovered that true fulfillment comes not from external markers of success, but from internal alignment with what matters. Later, his hard work paid off. As he started establishing his name in the sustainability world, he was offered a prestigious, well-paid job with a highly ranked business.

FINDING ACCEPTANCE AND HAPPINESS

Laila was 34 when she came to me complaining about finding herself constantly lost in others' shadow. She tended to mold herself to fit into someone else's shoes, believing that she'd finally find acceptance and happiness by doing so.

Laila's story is a common one. She admired her friends who seemed to have it all figured out—successful careers, fulfilling relationships, and seemingly unshakable confidence. She felt envious of their lives and yearned to be just like them.

One day, in a moment of self-reflection, Laila decided to take off those borrowed shoes and stand barefoot on her own path. The journey wasn't easy, but her quest for self-knowledge deepened her self-understanding, unearthed hidden talents, revealed her true passions, and illuminated her unique path.

Laila's transformation was striking. People began to notice the newfound confidence radiating from her. She no longer sought validation from others because she'd found it within herself.

Laila's story is a wake-up call to anybody who feels an emptiness inside their soul, disconnected from their dreams and desires. It's an honest invitation to connect with and honor your true self.

AUTHENTICITY IS THE MAIN DETERMINANT OF PERSONAL GROWTH

'THE PRIVILEGE OF A LIFETIME IS TO BECOME WHO YOU TRULY ARE.'

—CARL JUNG

You'll discover many benefits simply by becoming who you genuinely are. The above quote by Swiss psychiatrist Carl Jung (1875–1961) encourages individuals to recognize that authenticity and self-discovery are invaluable components of leading a meaningful life and that by staying true to ourselves, we unlock the potential for growth.

Autobiographies—including those of great leaders—are based on personal experiences, making them textbook examples of self-introspection and discovery. In each one, you'll find an account of the subject's personal struggles, trials and errors, observations, motives, feelings and actions, successes and failures, and lessons learned. By going through these diverse experiences, each individual forms the wisdom which informs who they are today. The more you know yourself, the more likely you'll live peacefully, achieve your goals, and gain self-confidence.

I invite you to start by writing your story—a mini-autobiography—on the blank page at the end of this chapter. Reflect on your life experiences, both past and present. Take your time thinking about significant events, crossroads, relationships, challenges, and moments of personal growth that have shaped you. Ask yourself, *What's my story?* Think about your social conditioning, family, community, and financial status. What has defined who you are today? By doing this, you're on your way to understanding your own motives, sentiments, and triggers.

What is authenticity?

'AUTHENTICITY IS THE DAILY PRACTICE OF LETTING GO OF WHO WE THINK WE ARE SUPPOSED TO BE AND EMBRACING WHO WE ARE.'

—BRENÉ BROWN

I won't say it requires daily practice, but authenticity involves at least a one-time decision to be yourself in a world that's persistently trying to shape you into somebody else—one that's consistently trying to prevent you from discovering your essence.

The power of being you is the challenge these days! With marketers continually leading you away from your essence, the constant feeling of inferiority, of being 'not enough', or of missing out, is the main driver behind our need to buy more, which (we think) will subdue our feelings of insufficiency!

BE HONEST AND INTROSPECTIVE

To start with, here are some questions you can ask yourself. Answer the first three to the best of your ability, ensuring you do this in a quiet room without interruptions. (Write down your answers on paper, because this will help you understand yourself better by facing your true values and desires.)

Go face to face with yourself when answering these questions:

1. What brings me the deepest sense of joy and fulfillment?
2. What are my core values, and how do they influence my decisions and actions? (Write between 10 and 25 core values, then choose your top three.)
3. What are my unique talents, strengths, and passions? (Enlist the help of parents and old friends.) When do you enter a 'flow state'? That's when you find yourself losing

track of time, too absorbed in what you're doing to even remember that you're hungry. So, what do you like spending time doing? What's your *ikigai*?
4. Am I living in alignment with my authentic self, or am I trying to please others or meet society's expectations?
5. What limiting beliefs or fears prevent me from expressing myself and pursuing my dreams?
6. How can I create more balance and harmony in my life?
7. What steps can I take to honor my needs and prioritize self-care?
8. What environments make me lose track of time and feel completely present and engaged?
9. How can I cultivate a deeper connection with my intuition? (Advanced)
10. What steps can I take to align my actions and goals with my desires?

The first three questions are crucial in revealing your *ikigai* and your flow state. The first prompts you to face reality, dig deep, and realize what the experiences or activities are that provide you with genuine happiness. This is best described by Mihaly Csikszentmihalyi in his book *Flow*, when talking about the characteristics of optimal experience and the clues as to how well an individual's performing:

> *Concentration is so intense that there is no attention left over to think about anything irrelevant, or to worry about problems. Self-consciousness disappears, and the sense of time becomes distorted. An activity that produces such experiences is so gratifying that people are willing to do it for its own*

sake, with little concern for what they will get out of it, even if it is difficult or dangerous.

This doesn't have to be hard. It can be making music, dancing, mountain climbing, playing chess, writing, thinking, or reading. Flow can also happen during family dinner, or when friends sit together and someone mentions a memory involving everyone in the gathering. Each person starts to remember, bringing a joke or story to the conversation. Soon, everyone's genuinely laughing, having fun, and feeling good about one another. Flow—the psychology of optimal experience—often results in situations such as this one.

Answering Question 1 to the best of your knowledge will be a life-changing starting point. From here on, you'll know your passion, what makes you happy, and how to enter a flow state.

Question 2, 'What are my core values?', is crucial to adjusting your compass in life. It's like tuning your purpose to the values you see as essential. For example, my top value is honesty. Everything else comes afterwards, including fidelity, family first, patience, faith in God, learning, and wisdom. Your list can include organization, helping others, listening, adaptability, resilience, continuity, focusing, and so on. Write up to 25 core values that are intensely important to you, then prioritize the most relevant three. After you've done this, you'll understand that your life, character, relationships, work, connections, family, and friends should all revolve around these three core values. Once you've clearly defined these, your whole life will improve.

In Question 3, we again pursue our individuality, talents, and strengths. This question is structured around three axes. The first involves your self-perspective. Do you see yourself as strong, intelligent, beautiful, sociable, loveable, or charismatic, for example? The second axis involves which subjects you got the best grades in at school and university. In which subjects did you outperform all your friends? What seems easy for you, yet difficult for others? Which topics cause you to become so intensely absorbed that you lose track of time and place? Which terms dominate your search history? What pages are you following on Instagram, YouTube, and so on? The third axis requires you to ask your closest family members and childhood friends the following questions: What are my strength points? What were my hobbies when I was young? What do you see in me that others might not? Answering this to the best of your knowledge will also be a turning point.

By now, you know who you are, your values, what you love, and what you're good at (your strength points). Your life's about to change, and your perspective on yourself is also changing for the better.

Now you're ready to answer Questions 4 and 5, which I refer to as *check-mates.* You must confront yourself: Am I living in alignment with who I truly am? Am I in harmony with my values? Do I know where my strength points lie? What are my unique talents? Am I utilizing them well? Confront yourself by checking which areas you're not performing in and why. Standing face to face with yourself, ask what's holding you back from reaching self-actualization. What do you fear? What are your limiting beliefs?

With the courage to question yourself and confront the reasons behind your fears, you'll liberate yourself from whatever's holding you back.

You're now in good shape to start your action plan. By answering Questions 6 to 10, you're establishing a step-by-step strategy to move into the future.

Why are these questions imperative?

These questions are tailored to extract optimal information about authenticity and essence. By answering them to the best of your capacity, you're learning what it means to be connected to yourself.

Still in doubt? Then let's further explore the idea of being disconnected from oneself. This state of being means high self-doubt, low self-esteem, a lack of purpose and meaning, and constant anxiety. This can also be reflected in physical terms, through unhealthy life choices, toxic relationships, and emotional instability. The story of Laila is a living example, demonstrating that only by walking in your own shoes, embracing your passions, and understanding your own worth can you unlock your highest potential and experience genuine happiness. Also, awakening your flow and *ikigai*—which I explain in the following section—is a state worth living in permanently.

WHAT IS *IKIGAI*?

The people of Japan believe that everyone has an *ikigai*—a reason to get out of bed each morning. As extracted from the international bestseller *Ikigai* by Hector Garcia and Francesc Miralles, it's the Japanese secret to a long and happy life (see Figure 4.1).

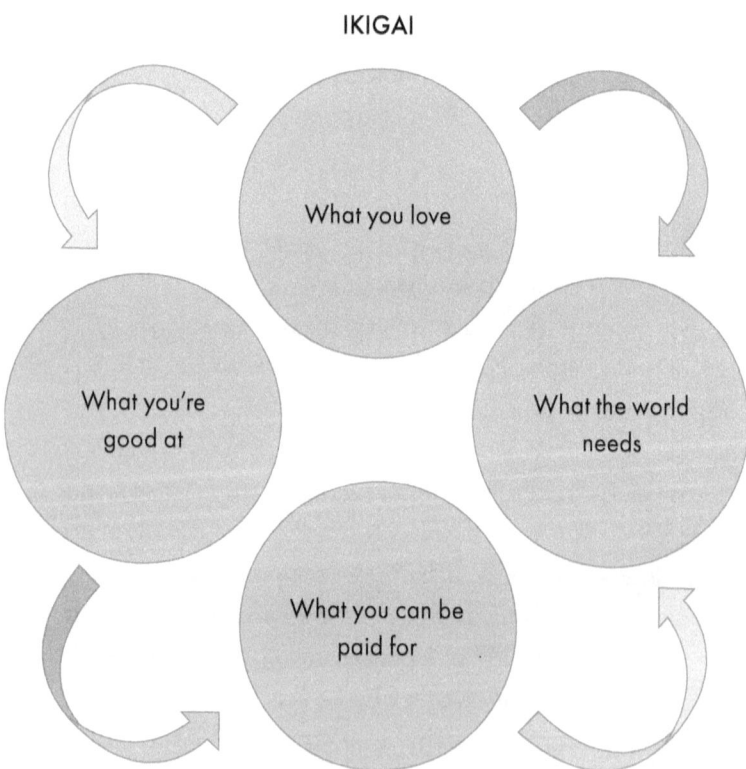

FIGURE 4.1: THE FOUR VALUES OF *IKIGAI*, PRODUCED FOR THIS BOOK.

Ikigai lies at the intersection between what you love, what you're good at, what the world needs, and what you can be paid for. The authors devised an equation whereby someone can connect with their passion and discover their mission, profession, and vocation, bringing meaning and joy to every day of their life.

This chapter may prompt some questions, which I've summarized as follows.

Q1: What if I'm too busy to pursue my passion?

A1: Don't underestimate the importance of knowing and pursuing your passion. By disconnecting from this part of yourself, you're cutting off a source of energy that introduces hope into your life. Not knowing your passion is a big mistake that Laila, my client, made by thinking that her choices would help her find acceptance; in fact, the opposite was true. She didn't fit in properly, and the more she tried, the emptier she felt. When Laila actively decided to understand herself, she discovered her hidden talents and unleashed her passion. Since then, she's led a more meaningful and fulfilling life, as well as attracting like-minded people. Deep down, she no longer experiences nagging emptiness.

Q2: What if I feel I have no strength points?

A2: If that's your view, you didn't do your work. Go back to the first three crucial questions in this chapter, take the time to answer them properly, then complete the rest. By doing this, you can form a holistic plan that will change your life and how you perceive what's around you. You'll then discover a greater sense of purpose, as well as inspiring others to question their own conformity.

Q3: Is it easy to get hold of my true self?

A3: Dare to be true to yourself, even if faced with societal pressures or the need to fit in. There are many examples of celebrities who struggle to express themselves through music, art, sports, or a certain solution to a specific problem. Determined to reconnect with their true passion, they stayed true to their unique vision despite facing setbacks and rejections. They found success by embracing their true selves, inspiring millions to embrace their uniqueness.

CHAPTER TAKEAWAYS

This chapter magnified the importance of tuning in to ourselves, which is a basic priority before connecting with others. Once we've reached a solid perception, everything else can be figured out. As explained in this chapter, many techniques can be used to get in touch with your true potential while understanding your weaknesses. Asking tailored questions, as well as practicing *ikigai* and flow, puts you in a better position to evaluate your deep-rooted desires, thus becoming a magnet for the joy you deserve.

Actions for readers

1. Open your mind and heart to who you really are. Here, you'll feel more comfortable, familiar, and in control. There's no need for lies, as everything's authentic. Progress can't be achieved without high levels of purity and authenticity.
2. Embrace yourself for who you are. As Oscar Wilde once said, 'Be yourself; everyone else is already taken.'
3. Remember that loving yourself is the basis of lifelong success. Striving to fly high? Start by accepting yourself, knowing your strength points, and learning your limitations. You'll have to face your limiting beliefs before starting your journey of self-discovery.

Finally, I'd like to wrap up this chapter with Rumi's elegant words:

'Do not feel lonely, the entire universe is inside you.'

WHAT'S NEXT?

Now we've accepted who we are, I'd like to talk about one of life's most important phenomena—*emotions*. Yes, emotions! They say intelligence quotient (IQ), and I say emotional quotient (EQ). IQ tests provide insight into intellectual capabilities, but don't measure qualities like creativity and emotional intelligence. Yet emotions are integral to our being, and shouldn't be surpassed, ignored, or left undealt with. We need to understand them, face them, and have power over them.

In the coming chapter, you'll learn all you need to know about emotions and how they impact our belief systems and actions. You will learn how to take control of them. Finally, remember that by controlling your emotions, you control your life.

YOUR SPACE

Chapter 5

- FIND YOUR PURPOSE
- TUNE IN TO THE 'TRUE YOU'
- **UNDERSTAND YOUR EMOTIONAL STATE** ← *We are here*
- ACCEPT THE POWER OF QUESTIONS AND WORDS
- UTILIZE THE POWER OF FOCUS
- EMBRACE PAIN
- TAKE ACTION

CHAPTER 5

THE POWER OF EMOTIONS

Understand the Nature of Your Feelings
and the Magnitude of Your Sentiments

What if I told you that emotions have the power to shape your whole life and destiny? They're the hidden force behind all successes in life. Yet they also constitute the unseen drive behind all failures and deceptions. Emotions can bring you health and wealth and can attract anything that you desire in life. However, this same tool can repel happiness and bring misery, despair, and hardship into your life.

This chapter is an open invitation for you to understand the nature and magnitude of your emotions. It will help you unlock the hidden messages that different emotions are signaling to you.

By the end of this chapter, you'll be able to comprehend your negative emotions. Moreover, you'll learn the positive purpose they serve. Emotions such as anger, frustration, sadness, anxiety, fear, boredom, embarrassment, disappointment, being overwhelmed, or even feelings of loneliness and helplessness, all call on you to take actions that bring about a better quality of life. For example, boredom can call on you to take outside-the-box action, and this in turn can lead to new inventions, artistic endeavors, and so on. Feelings of loneliness can call on you to seek your hobbies, or to connect with your friends, family and so on.

This chapter will deepen your familiarity with the term 'emotional intelligence' and teach you how to manage your own emotions and those of others, thus strengthening your self-awareness, self-regulation, empathy, and even your communication skills.

Identifying and interpreting your emotions is the first step to wellbeing and mental health. Being able to flow with and control your emotions will give you more power to control your life. Do you remember a time when you couldn't curb your emotions and thus lost your battle in a particular situation?

How about the opposite? Do you remember a situation where you controlled your emotions and triumphed during a struggle?

Last but not least, emotions significantly impact our thoughts, belief systems, behavior, and overall wellbeing. Emotions influence decision-making. They can confer strength and motivation, build relationships, and greatly impact your physical health.

WHAT IS THE DEFINITION OF 'EMOTION'?

To simplify the concept, let's define it.

Emotions are complex psychological states triggered by external events, internal thoughts, or physiological changes in the body. They involve subjective feelings, behavioral responses, and physiological reactions.

Emotions strongly influence how individuals perceive and respond to their environment, affecting their thoughts, behaviors, and overall health states. Common emotions include joy, love, sadness, confusion, depression, anger, fear, jealousy, and disgust.

The five steps to emotional mastery

Here's a five-step process for emotional mastery, which can be used whenever distressing or hurtful negative emotions arise. Following these steps will help you acknowledge the emotion you're experiencing and understand its message, enabling you to take appropriate action to avoid pain or suffering and direct your life toward favorable outcomes.

Step 1:

Identify the emotion

Ask yourself direct questions to pinpoint what you're really feeling.

Am I feeling lonely? Am I feeling bored? Am I feeling hurt? Is it pain that I'm feeling, or am I just in a bad mood? By asking yourself such questions, you lower the emotional intensity and start to understand what that specific emotion signals. Consider these emotions as messages reaching out to you, trying to provide useful firsthand information about your state.

All you have to do is learn from that emotion as if you're talking to your toddler—you're trying to declutter the overwhelming and confusing nature of emotions to reach deep into the core reason for their upsetting presence.

Once you know what you're feeling, write it down as confirmation of your acknowledgment. For example, you can write 'I'm feeling lonely,' 'I'm feeling frustrated,' 'I'm feeling envious,' 'I'm embarrassed,' and so on. Here, we're trying to pinpoint the problem, the state we're in, or simply the emotions we're feeling. This will make it easier to deal with and learn from the situation.

Step 2:

Recognize that emotions are here to support you

Trust your emotions; they're here to support and guide you. Emotions are never wrong. Any emotion works as an alert until you do something about it, or in other words, until you take action to solve it. Maybe *loneliness* signals that it's time to call your friends, ask about your family, or become more extroverted. Boredom informs you that it's the right time to pursue your hobbies. Depression calls on you to renew your hope and motivation, to do something to solve it, and so on.

What you feel is what you feel—there's no mistaking it!

Be grateful for all your emotional states, even if you don't understand them as they flow. There will come a moment when they'll all make sense to you. All your emotions are here for you to use as a tool to make positive adjustments.

Step 3:

Learn the message that the emotion is conveying

Get excited about trying to figure out the *aim* of this emotion. Maybe that feeling of disappointment is trying to tell you that you haven't done what you should. It's trying to propel you to go back and take appropriate action in a specific situation.

Smith, one of my clients, came to me one day feeling sad, frustrated, and annoyed. First, I asked him to identify what he was really feeling. Feeling confused, Smith didn't know why he was feeling down and lacking energy. All he knew was that he was overwhelmed by bitterness, sorrow, and unhappiness. I asked him to sit back and tell me honestly what he was feeling at that moment. He then confided his feelings: 'Right now, I feel angry.' At this point, Smith identified with his exact emotion. This helped lower its intensity and made it easier for both of us to deal with, learn from, and extract the message his anger was trying to convey.

Step 4:

Recall techniques that can often help you get over a negative emotion

Writing down everything you feel inside will help you understand and heal from the negative emotions you're trapped by. For example, you could write, 'I'm feeling frustrated and pressured because I have too much work to do, and I'm afraid I won't meet the deadlines.' Or, 'I feel embarrassed because my presentation at the meeting was bad.' Or, 'I feel envious, as my colleague got promoted and I wasn't.' The truer to yourself you are, the closer you'll be to identifying and understanding your true emotions, how you're feeling, and why. Eventually, it becomes easy to break down the emotion and change your mood for the better.

Writing down your feelings and the related event will help you when you need to recall a situation where you overcame your negative emotions. What did you do? Smith remembered that when he usually feels angry, he steps back, remains silent, and sleeps on it. He tries to get involved in other activities, such as walking in nature, listening to his favorite songs, engaging in social activities, or seeing a movie. All of these activities change his mood and lower the intensity of his feelings.

Step 5:

Take action

Don't remain stuck because of your restrictive emotions. Instead, express yourself, identify the emotions, and understand the message they're trying to convey. By understanding your emotions—especially the negative ones—you are lowering their intensity, thus decreasing the impact and power they have over you. Afterwards you get the clarity to deal with them and take the right action.

Working closely with Smith, we identified his intense feelings of anger. He felt irritated, uncomfortable, and, at times, furious. We worked on trusting his emotions and even feeling grateful for them, because they served a purpose. Smith understood that he'd violated a value that was important to him by insulting his colleague at work, who became deeply offended. Being rude to people is simply not part of Smith's ethical standard.

Feeling bad about himself, Smith recognized that his strong feelings of distress and embarrassment were telling him to refine his actions. Smith understood that he couldn't tolerate offending his colleague, as being nice to people is one of Smith's major values.

He immediately took the phone and called his colleague. He sincerely apologized for being rude to him and promised that this would never happen again. His colleague felt better; day after day, he started to forgive Smith and respect the courage behind his apology.

This obviously had an instant impact on the way Smith felt about himself. Since then, Smith has learned how to identify and acknowledge his feelings. He's learned to analyze and understand the messages behind his emotions and to take the necessary actions.

Every time you notice confusing or perplexing emotions, using this framework will help you to pinpoint the emotion and then get over it. This will give you the power to change your mood instantly, or at least decrease the intensity of your emotional state (see Figure 5.1).

The 5 steps to emotional mastery

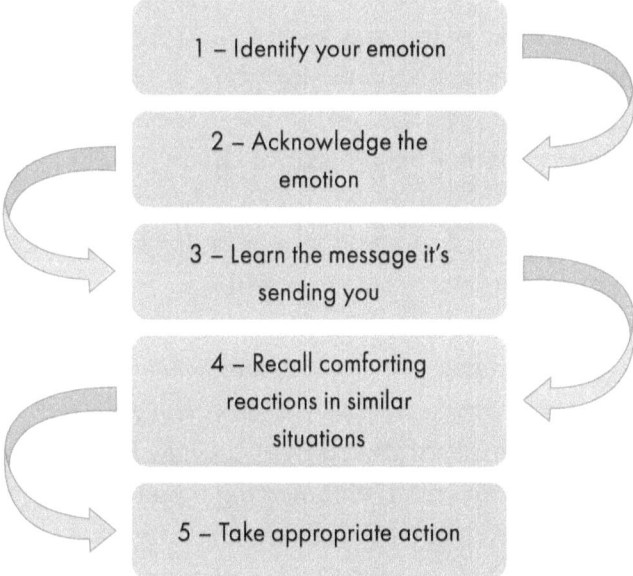

FIGURE 5.1: THE 5 STEPS TO EMOTIONAL MASTERY.

Through this step-by-step approach, you can lower the intensity of any negative emotion experienced in future. You'll also be able to curb any resentful emotion while using it as a call to action.

Throughout life's ups and downs, emotions play a vital role in rendering life more colorful and 'alive'. On a deeper level, emotions shape our thoughts and behaviors, from anger to joy, anxiety to security, loneliness to familiarity, and pain to tranquility. Don't resent your emotions. On the contrary, treat them as seasons, as they come and go, yet make us feel alive!

It all starts with your emotional state. If you master your emotions, you master your life—that is, your health and wealth at home and work. Some may even say, 'Your success in life depends on your *emotional* intelligence.'

So far, we've learned how negative emotions try to send us positive messages and drive us to act. What follows are 10 negative emotions that are common in daily life, along with the messages they are trying to reveal.

In his amazing book, *Awaken the giant within: Take immediate control of your mental, emotional, physical and financial destiny*, Anthony Robbins lists the ten most prevalent negative emotions and how each sends empowering messages and calls to action. In the following table, I've summarized the spectrum of negative emotions and the call to action behind each one (see Figure 5.2).

The Emotion	The Message
Discomfort	Something's not quite right.
Fear	Be prepared.
Hurt	You have an unmet expectation.
Anger	An important value in your life has been violated by someone else (or even by yourself).
Frustration	Your brain believes that you could be doing better than you currently are.
Disappointment	An expectation you have probably isn't going to happen.
Guilt	You've violated one of your highest standards, and must do something immediately to ensure this won't happen again.
Inadequacy	You don't presently have the level of skill needed to accomplish the task at hand.
Overload or Overwhelm	You need to reevaluate your priorities in this situation.
Loneliness	You need to form connections with people.

FIGURE 5.2: THE MOST COMMON NEGATIVE EMOTIONS AND THEIR MEANINGS.

Each of these emotions is trying to alert you to something that's not going well, and tell you that you need to take a specific course of action. This is true for the whole span of emotions, from mild discomfort to intense feelings of guilt and disappointment. You can add to the list as many emotions as you feel, then seek the meaning each is persuading you with. In this context, emotions are acting as a catalyst that seek to provide you with a message!

For example, discomfort can signal boredom, distress, unease, or embarrassment. Maybe you're impatient, or your actions aren't producing the required results. To work this out, try a different approach, which you'll adjust through trial and error to produce the desired results. Remember that it can persist and intensify if you don't deal with the emotion at its roots.

Another bitter emotion is fear, interpreted as a strong feeling of worry. It can even translate into anxiety and a persistent obsession that something bad will happen. In the real world, 99 percent of what we fear most never happens. We don't want to surrender to our fears, nor do we want to pretend they don't exist. However, there's a middle ground that enables you to assess the situation you're fearful about and take appropriate action while having faith that you've done your best.

Hurt is another harsh emotion that can reach high intensities. This can manifest on many levels, reaching grief, agony, anger, suffering, pain, or even depression. It should be tackled with maximum care; otherwise, the pain can develop into irreversible scars. Hurt should be dealt with at its deepest roots and solved correctly and immediately. Alternatively, it can be left to mend over time. It will take longer, but it will definitely heal.

Anger and frustration are strong emotions that might lead to disappointment, one of the most devastating outcomes. Anger, in its most intense forms, can be manifested when deception is perpetrated, and the result can be permanent. Examples of deception range from dishonesty to betrayal. You know that the impact can last forever. The best way to deal with such setbacks is to have faith and to learn the lessons behind the event.

Last but not least are the emotions of guilt and remorse—two of the most potent emotions, which are related but with distinct differences. Guilt typically refers to a feeling of responsibility or regret for something we have done or failed to do, resulting in a sense of self-blame and condemnation. On the other hand, remorse goes beyond guilt. It involves a deeper emotional response that includes regret, sorrow, and empathy for the hurt and harm caused to others. It encompasses a more profound sense of responsibility and a desire to make amends or seek forgiveness.

Remorse involves not only acknowledging the wrongdoing, but also feeling sorry for the impact it had on others. Guilt may lead to remorse when individuals acknowledge the full extent of their actions and genuinely seek to learn from their mistakes and repair the harm caused. Thomas Mondel described this well: 'Regret and remorse are among the emotions human beings do most to avoid in life.' Meanwhile, this feeling of remorse can hold great value in the future, as it's the most powerful tool that guarantees you'll never repeat the same mistake. In other words, it cuts a bad deed out at its roots. As you know deep inside that what you did was wrong, you sign a secret contract with yourself to ensure it never happens again.

Feeling guilt is the ultimate tool to change a behavior entirely and permanently. Tony Robbins explains the purpose of guilt:

He believes guilt can serve a constructive purpose when it motivates us to acknowledge our mistakes, make amends, and strive to improve our behavior.

The other extreme is to surrender and wallow in guilt, where we begin to just accept the pain and experience learned helplessness. This is not the purpose of guilt. Again, it is designed to drive us to create a change. People fail to understand this, often feeling so remorseful about something they once did that they allow themselves to feel inferior for the rest of their lives!

For this part, and due to the important role emotions play in our personal and professional lives, I've dedicated the following section to answering questions that might have popped up as you were reading this pivotal chapter.

Q1: What if I can't pinpoint any negative emotion coming my way?

A1: By now, you should be able to identify any bad emotion you're feeling. Moreover, you should feel positive and excited about it, as you know it's here to serve a purpose. Start by connecting with how you're feeling and why. Write down on paper, 'I'm feeling …' The more you write, the clearer your feelings will become. If you're still confused, sleep on it and get involved in other activities until the situation clears up or your feelings become less intense. This will allow you to better understand the emotion and get through it.

In all cases, be mindful, curious, and even excited about understanding the message the negative emotion is trying to communicate. Otherwise, it will continue running after you until the message finally gets through.

Q2: What if I can't handle the emotion at hand? In other words, I know how I feel, but I'm overwhelmed and can't take immediate or direct action.

A2: Sometimes, we feel so overwhelmed by the emotion that we think the problem's too big to handle. We can even believe that things are simply outside our control. In this situation, the best thing to do is calm down and distract your mind by doing something you love, such as getting involved in a different activity, playing with your kids, going for a walk, or reading a book—whatever you like to do. You can even go further by helping others solve their problems. Any of these actions have the power to distract your attention from the issue you're currently overwhelmed by, thus clearing your mind so you can take a fresh look at the problem and reevaluate your priorities.

Another way to counter-attack the negative emotion is to replace it with a positive one, like love, gratitude, curiosity, excitement, and determination. These empowering emotions can efficiently turn the situation upside-down.

By handling and mastering your emotions, you can grasp the positive side of any negative situation, the opportunity arising from any challenge, and the lesson to extract from any problem.

Q3: What's the difference between emotional quotient (EQ) and intelligence quotient (IQ)?

A3: The message I'm trying to pass on to you in this chapter is stronger and more powerful than anything else someone can learn. Your emotional intelligence is a major determinant of your success in life, unlike IQ, which measures a person's intelligence compared to others. IQ involves reasoning, problem-solving, memory, and other cognitive skills. EQ is a person's ability to recognize, understand, manage, and express emotions effectively. This also involves awareness, empathy, mindfulness, interpersonal skills, and self-control. The main difference between IQ and EQ lies in the types of intelligence they measure. IQ focuses on cognitive abilities and analytical thinking, while EQ centers on emotional awareness and social skills.

Both IQ and EQ are important in different aspects of life. The latter—EQ—has been underestimated for many decades, only to return to the spotlight and become a central element in determining any person's professional and personal success. We also can't underestimate its importance in predicting mental health and wellbeing. In conclusion, emotional mastery is a crucial foundation for individuals' happiness, and ultimately for community and societal success.

CHAPTER TAKEAWAYS

It's crucial to understand that whichever emotion occurs to you, whether good or bad, depends on the meaning you give to it. Give it a bad name, and you suffer; give it a good name, and you move your life to the next level. In conclusion, whatever emotion you have, whether negative or positive, depends upon your understanding of its meaning.

Whenever you feel down, ask yourself, 'What else could this mean?' Asking this question is the first step toward liberating yourself from the hold that bad emotions have over you. The best takeaway I want to instill in you from this chapter is this:

By controlling your emotions, you control your life!

Actions for readers

- Learn to control your emotions so they don't control you; also, learn what hidden messages emotions are trying to trigger in you, so you can take the right action.

Finally, don't underestimate your feelings. What you feel is true; you just need to identify it, understand it, and work through it.
- Whenever you feel any intense emotion, such as hurt, deceit, or betrayal, or the less intense emotions, such as discomfort or sadness, go back to the 5-step system to emerge from your emotional state full of energy. This system will help you develop the confidence and understanding to get over the emotion and use it in your favor.
- Grasp each emotion's positive hidden messages, then stand back on your feet again—this time, you'll be more grounded and much stronger than before. That's what I call *emotional resilience*.

WHAT'S NEXT?

This leads us to the next chapter, where we'll discuss the importance and the power of questions in more detail. Asking smart questions will get you smart answers, and asking the right questions will get you the right answers.

Get ready to delve into the world of asking yourselves and others better questions and using the power of words. By asking yourself better questions, you open your way to a better quality of life, and by choosing kind words, you profoundly impact yourselves and others.

YOUR SPACE

Chapter 6

| FIND YOUR PURPOSE |

| TUNE IN TO THE 'TRUE YOU' |

| UNDERSTAND YOUR EMOTIONAL STATE |

| ACCEPT THE POWER OF QUESTIONS AND WORDS | ← We are here

| UTILIZE THE POWER OF FOCUS |

| EMBRACE PAIN |

| TAKE ACTION |

CHAPTER 6

THE POWER OF QUESTIONS

Mastering the Art of Internal and External Communication to Transform Your Life

I think by now, you would've started wondering what the secret behind unstoppable growth and success is. The secret lies in your ability to continuously use your silent weapons—questions and words.

A curious mind is a great sign of intelligence, persistence, and a deep willingness to understand and search for authentic truth. You reach a higher stage of certainty and truth through questioning or doubting.

I don't know a more powerful yet simple technique to achieve your goals than the power of questions. Questions are the basis of any plan. If you have an objective to achieve, what's the first step? You simply start by asking the right questions. The sequence of your answers will get you where you want to be.

Questions are basic tools that reflect a need to clarify something and a need for adequate and accurate answers. For example, you need to know your life goal, so you ask a direct question: 'What's my ultimate purpose or goal in life?' You need to gain clarity, so you ask more questions: 'Why do I need that?' 'How do I do it?' and 'How do I start from this point?' The possibilities are endless. You ask the *how* ('How do I go about doing this?'), then you go back and investigate the *what if* ('What if I fail?' 'What if I don't reach that goal?' 'What would happen then?' 'What's the cost?' 'Is it worth it?' or 'What's the worst-case scenario?'). These are mental calculations and risk evaluations that the mind undertakes to guide you through achieving your goals. All of this mental work begins with a question that we address to ourselves in a sincere attempt to study the situation and find a way through it.

Throughout this chapter, you'll learn not only the power of questions but also the power of words. You'll discover the rules of the so-called *success vocabulary*—the words you need to affirm to yourself—so that you can reassure yourself that you're about to win. You'll learn how questions work, as well as their different types: empowering, problem-solving, and happiness-related. At the end of the chapter, there's a bonus question: the 'one-million-dollar destiny' question.

Stay tuned, remembering Tony Robbins's insight that 'It is not only the questions you ask, but the questions you fail to ask, that shape your destiny.'

THE IMPORTANCE OF QUESTIONS

As I wrote this chapter, I was keen to highlight the significance of *questions* in fueling curiosity, stimulating critical thinking, and encouraging learning and growth. I was struggling to put the first few words into the book until I asked myself three questions:

- Why am I writing this book?
- Who is this book for?
- What problem does it solve?

In the answers, I found my words, my calling, and the reason this book is out there. I'm sharing this case to show how questions can be productive in achieving clarity of thought and helping an individual hit their goal or target.

Did you know that most people are hesitant or afraid to ask questions, specifically the right ones? They don't want to face the right answers. They don't dare to question the status quo. They don't have the courage to reach out for truths that, if tackled, might change their whole existence. Truth can sometimes hurt, but without questioning, doubting, and assessing, there's no growth or development!

Questions are fundamental to opening the doors to new opportunities, perspectives, and knowledge. They're the gateway to all new learning.

Above all, questions open our eyes to new discoveries, and thus new horizons. I'm not exaggerating when I say that even a child's success in life can be measured from an early age through their curiosity, questions, and mindset. He who doesn't question the world around him has a fixed mindset.

Throughout this book, we'll learn how our beliefs affect our thoughts, decisions, actions—and consequently, our destiny.

I believe it all lies in the way we think.

As a matter of fact, *The Way You Think* was the first title I chose for this book! 😊

It's little wonder, since the questions you ask determine the quality of your thoughts. As the great philosopher Voltaire (François-Marie Arouet) once said when addressing the significance and weight of questions, 'Judge a man by his questions rather than his answers.'

What is a question?

Let's start by defining *question*. My definition of a question is a deep-seated one. A question is a mind game where you dig deep into your mind to find the missing pieces of a puzzle so that the mind can form a bigger picture of what it needs to know. Most often, something is missing, and the mind is lost in its pursuit of the truth. The more questions you ask, the closer you get to the truth.

Smart questions can play a pivotal role as disruptors to the system

If you're a professional life coach, you know that your job is 80 percent listening; the remaining 20 percent relies on asking the right questions.

In reality, it's not only the questions you asked yourself that shaped your life but also the questions you *failed* to ask. In the end, when we look back on our life, it's the things we didn't do and the decisions we didn't take that we'll regret most.

Questions are game-changers, and if you take the chance to ask yourself the right question at the right time—even if it seems difficult or embarrassing—you'll have the privilege of advancing in your journey toward fulfillment. It's in the answers that we find our way through.

As we mentioned before, all kinds of questions are analytical; we're inquiring to find clarity and hidden truths out of each question. There's an array of different types of questions. Questions can be problem-solving, exploratory (to discover new situations, explore new horizons, or sense new possibilities for growth), or even *self*-exploratory. They can also be explanatory, to further investigate an issue or clarify matters.

Questions can also be used as affirmations, as well as for self-help. It's no wonder private investigators use many types of questioning techniques to get to the truth. Undoubtedly, the better the questions, the better the answers. Some questions are so smart that we can't escape the bright side of the answer. That's why judging a person by their questions, not their answers, is a plausible strategy.

The destiny question

We've been talking about the power of questions as a tool to reach clarity and achieve success. Ten years ago a friend of mine, who's also a life coach, looked directly into my eyes and asked the destiny question: 'Where do you see yourself in the next 10 years?' This was bitterly challenging for me, because I knew by then exactly where I wanted to see myself in the next decade. However, I was afraid to answer, and hesitant to take the required road to reach where I should be today.

She kept asking the same question, but in many different ways, for example: 'Ten years from now, what is that thing that you would regret the most if not accomplished?' and 'Where do you see yourself in the next five years?' The questions were so disruptive that I felt extremely uncomfortable answering them.

Have you ever had that feeling of knowing what you want, yet you simply couldn't do it? You feel as if you've been shackled with iron. The questions were so upsetting to me that to answer them, I had to gather all of my courage and face the blatant truth I was hiding from. Trembling, I responded:

'Yes, I know what I *should* be achieving 10 years from now, but I simply can't do it—or honestly speaking, I don't have the courage to do it.'

She stood right in front of me, annoyed, and replied loudly, 'Excuse me, what do you lack that causes you to kill your dream and not do what you should be doing? What do you lack that causes you to prevent yourself from feeling happiness and fulfillment? What do you lack that causes you to not become who you should become?'

We sat together and sorted everything out. We identified and eliminated my limiting beliefs—those about myself and those about society and others—and put together short- and long-term plans. Together, we organized the steps to achieve my future goals, and that was it. I exerted all the required efforts in the most gracious and authentic way, and guess what?

First, thanks to God, I had the courage to answer that million-dollar question, and now (after 10 years), I find myself in the exact place I should be with the life I should be leading and the status I should have. Moreover, I haven't missed the golden opportunity to answer my life's calling and achieve my dreams.

This smart question was asked at the right time, and I was prepared. It did it all! It brought about the required change in my life. It gave me the clarity to reach out for new horizons.

It challenged my assumptions, reevaluated what I thought was beyond my capabilities, and helped me recognize my strength points to work things out. It propelled me to visualize the kind of life I should be leading. This type of question was so provocative to me that it compelled me to rediscover and reinvent myself again and again.

Since then, I've worked hard on making the impossible possible, and my dreams come to fruition.

Can you imagine how an intriguing question can become a game-changer and turn your whole life upside-down in the most beautiful way? It happened to me, and it can definitely happen to anyone.

30 questions in coaching

Following is a table of the 30 most thought-provoking questions used in life coaching. These questions are well-studied. They're designed to stimulate people to face their own realities, desires, and needs, to confront their fears and limiting beliefs, and to understand the reasons behind not reaching their goals. These questions are powerful tools for understanding the exact price and value of the required change (see Figure 6.1).

#	Type	The Question
1-	Goal setting	Where do you want to see yourself in the next 10 years?
2-	Goal setting	What will you regret the most if not accomplished in 10 years' time?
3-	Goal setting	What do you want to achieve in the next five years?
4-	Values	In one word, what's your most important goal in life?
5-	Goals	In one sentence, what's the most important topic for you this year?
6-	Values	In one word, what's the most valuable asset you own right now?
7-	Alignment	In one sentence, who are you today and who do you want to become?
8-	Truth	What's missing in your life?
9-	Affirmation	Why do you want to achieve that goal?
10-	Affirmation	How does it feel to accomplish this goal?
11-	Affirmation	What would your life look like after achieving this goal?
12-	Reasoning	What compromises do you need to make to achieve that goal?
13-	Reasoning	Are you ready to make these compromises to achieve your goal?
14-	Reasoning	Is the goal worth it?
15-	Daring	Can you visualize your life when you've achieved your dream/goal?
16-	Truth	What challenges will you have to face to achieve your dream?

#	Type	The Question
17-	Confrontation	What's holding you back from achieving your goal? What are your limiting beliefs?
18-	Truth	What other areas in your life will be affected by achieving your goal?
19-	Confrontation	What's the price of achieving this goal?
20-	Challenging	Are you ready to pay it?
21-	Confrontation	Does this goal fit within your current priorities and lifestyle?
22-	Confrontation	How will your daily life look after achieving your goal?
23-	Daring	Why do you think this goal is important? Why do you think you deserve it?
23-	Predictions	How will your life be better with this goal achieved?
24-	Action plan	Who do you need, to achieve your goal.
25-	Analytical	What needs to be changed for you to achieve your goal?
26-	Analytical	Do you know any person(s) who has achieved your dream/goal already? Name a person who achieved what you long for.
27-	Analytical	What can you learn from them?
28-	Implementation	What steps do you need to take right now to get where you want to be in the future?
29-	Weighing	What gains will you reap by taking this decision?
30-	Crossroad	What will happen if you don't choose to take that crossroad now? How will your life be 10 years from now?

FIGURE 6.1: 30 QUESTIONS IN COACHING.

It's natural to have needs and desires. The problem arises when we don't acknowledge them. We think it's unacceptable to have any wants or needs. Rationally, if those demands aren't met, distress and unhappiness prevail, persisting until those needs are fulfilled.

This is why the more you acknowledge your needs and the clearer your goals and intentions, the higher the probability you'll be satisfied.

A life coach may work gradually through the spectrum of questions, starting with simple questions like, 'What do you want in life?', 'What kind of person would you like to be?', 'What are your goals?', 'What are the changes you'd like to make?', and 'Are you ready for these changes?', before moving to thought-based questions, like 'Are your thoughts generally positive or negative?', 'What are the questions you ask yourself?' 'What beliefs and deep-rooted values control your life?', 'What are you trying to reach out for by thinking this way?', and so on.

As the fastest way to your subconscious mind, imagination can bring your needs into a three-dimensional world. By learning to respect your intuition and use creative visualization, you can imagine achieving your dreams and how you'd like your life to look. The last tool to use in the life coaching journey is taking action and overcoming your fears. Even if you're only taking small steps in the right direction, it will be enough to get you through.

By answering and reflecting on the questions in Figure 6.1, you'll allow yourself to understand your deep desires and goals, which, in turn, will improve the quality of your life once achieved. Answering these questions is also the first step in achieving them. By highlighting and giving yourself the gift of knowing and aligning with your soul's calling, you're 50 percent of the way there, if not more.

THE STORY OF TAMARA

Tamara, a former colleague, was in her early forties when she reached out to me. One day, she came to me distressed and miserable. In a sad voice, she said, 'I have been treated unfairly, stabbed in the back and betrayed. People are becoming so inhumane at the workplace. I feel I don't belong, especially after I wasn't promoted and the promotion went to a junior, recently hired employee.'

The story of Tamara happens every day. I listened carefully and then asked her kindly, 'Tamara, in all your life, how many people have let you down? How many people have hurt you and left a deep wound in your feelings?' She paused for quite some time to count, and then, trembling, she said, 'Around three or four, maximum.' I confirmed, 'In your whole life?' She replied, 'Yes, exactly.' So, again, I asked gently, 'Tamara, how many people have helped you, supported you, had your back, lifted you up when you were down, smiled at you, and were kind to you?' Tamara smiled at once and said, 'Maybe one hundred or one thousand ... there are so many, I can't count!' At this point, the subject was closed forever.

Tamara was always clever, and quickly grasped the message behind my question. Believe it or not, one question could distract her attention, direct her to think better, and dig deep to access the truths in her life. One smart question immediately changed how she felt and the state and intensity of her emotions.

As we approach the end of this chapter, I'll address some questions that might have arisen at this point:

Q1: I have fears about facing reality and being asked difficult questions that directly hit my pain points.

A1: Smart questions are one of the strongest tools that will force you to look inward and face your own fears and realities. The moment you're forced or compelled to confront your pain points is *exactly* the moment you acknowledge that you have a problem and you decide to solve it.

It's undeniable that the moment you accept you have a problem and start solving it, you can put your fears aside and be sure that facing the truth—even if it's painful—is a far better option than hiding from it. Facing your fears is the beginning of solving the problem and creating a new and better reality for yourself.

Q2: **I know my pain point, but I can't help touching it, discussing it, or even coming closer to it.**

A2: That is where the help of a professional life coach is so valuable in addressing the issue and the suffering without hurting you. A professional life coach will highlight and activate your strengths while addressing your weaknesses, working on both to reevaluate your most persistent needs and demands, thus reaching your goals while being supported.

People who deny themselves the right to have demands in life suffer from persistent unhappiness and may live in consistent despair. There are moral and psychological needs, like the desire to grow, progress, develop, achieve success, and improve our life. There's a need for security, power, a need to love and be loved, and a need to connect with others and God.

All these desires are legitimate, and acknowledging their existence is important. The more your own needs are met, the happier you'll be. Likewise, the opposite holds true: The less your demands are met, the more desperate and miserable you'll be.

This is illustrated clearly in Maslow's Hierarchy of Needs, created by American psychologist Abraham Maslow (1908–1970). His theory of psychological health is predicated on fulfilling innate human needs in order of priority, culminating in self-actualization.

Maslow's argument emphasizes the significance of meeting the most basic needs before people can move up the hierarchy to meet more advanced ones. (For a more detailed description of the pattern through which human needs and motivations generally move, here is a useful link to learn more about Maslow's Hierarchy of Needs: https://www.simplypsychology.org/maslow.html)

Q3: Talking about the power of questions, how about the power of words? What possible impact can they have on our daily experiences, happiness, and success?

A3: The words we speak, think, and believe every day of our lives are powerful and greatly impact our daily mood and subsequently, our cumulative experience. If you have optimistic and encouraging thoughts in general, they'll have a positive impact on your quality of life.

On the other hand, if you have negative thoughts for one day, it doesn't mean you're depressed. However, having negative thoughts for long enough *can* create a miserable life, offering a place for depression to lay down its roots.

Words are our main tool for communicating, getting along, understanding, interpreting, and translating each other's emotions. You can guess how powerful the names we give to our experiences are. Then, these labels can directly alter the sensations generated within our nervous systems. Words directly impact our biochemistry. As the Persian poet Hafiz once said, 'The words we speak become the house we live in.'

CHAPTER TAKEAWAYS

Of all the people we meet in our daily lives, I bet those who are really successful are the ones who ask smart questions, even to themselves. They're the ones who dare to answer even the most intriguing and disruptive questions—those who choose their words carefully, who always use positive words, and who practice affirmative self-talk. Choosing kind words when communicating with others also greatly impacts their quality of life. As we always say, 'Be careful with your words; they can be forgiven but never forgotten.'

> Be CAREFUL of your THOUGHTS, for your THOUGHTS become your WORDS.
>
> Be CAREFUL OF YOUR WORDS, for your WORDS become your ACTIONS.
>
> Be CAREFUL OF YOUR ACTIONS, for your ACTIONS become your HABITS.
>
> Be CAREFUL OF YOUR HABITS, for your HABITS become your CHARACTER.
>
> Be CAREFUL OF YOUR CHARACTER, for your CHARACTER becomes your DESTINY.

Actions for readers

1. Dare to ask questions, as 'He who asks questions cannot avoid the answers.' This beautifully expressed Cameroonian proverb reflects the cultural values and wisdom of continuously asking questions so that we can't avoid progressing in the right direction. Ask intelligent, directed questions, and you'll challenge assumptions and break the limits of your ability to learn. By embracing the importance of questions, you grow personally and intellectually.

2. For more resources about the power of words, visit my YouTube channel, Hoda Elsobky (www.youtube.com/@hodaelsobky8984) and search for the episode on Al Dafrah TV on the value of *trust* and how words can build or break it. Or you can simply go to the following link: https://youtu.be/T_AFfBMekmk?si=zOzr9ZHbIBLVc2Wm

   Don't forget to subscribe to my channel!

3. Whenever faced with ambiguity of the mind, start by asking questions to clear the way through and gain clarity in your thoughts.

   Asking the right questions clears out old conditioning (such as thought patterns), making way for new ideas and thoughts. By mastering this skill, you elevate your decision-making ability and reach a higher quality of life.

WHAT'S NEXT?

This leads us to the next important tool in our diagram: *the power of focus* and why it matters. We'll learn to become more focused and effective in a world full of agitations and interferences. How to concentrate so that we can easily unleash our own creativity and out-of-the-box modes of thinking. How to revive our own alertness and energies to concurrent tasks or problems, and how to focus on the end result so that we can't avoid achieving it.

YOUR SPACE

Chapter 7

- FIND YOUR PURPOSE
- TUNE IN TO THE 'TRUE YOU'
- UNDERSTAND YOUR EMOTIONAL STATE
- ACCEPT THE POWER OF QUESTIONS AND WORDS
- UTILIZE THE POWER OF FOCUS ← *We are here*
- EMBRACE PAIN
- TAKE ACTION

CHAPTER 7

THE POWER OF FOCUS

Harnessing Your Mental Energy for Success

In a world filled with endless distractions and constant multitasking, the ability to focus has become a rare and precious commodity. Imagine what you could achieve if you could eliminate the background noise holding you back, utilize the power of your mind to accomplish your goals, realize your dreams, and make them all come true.

Research shows that the average person's attention span has dwindled to a mere eight seconds, shorter than that of a goldfish. In our fast-paced digital age, we've become experts at flitting from one task to another, never fully committing to any single endeavor. The dire consequences of this divided attention are evident in our personal and professional lives, as opportunities slip through our fingers and our dreams remain unfulfilled.

TIME TO BREAK THE VICIOUS CYCLE

It's time to change things for the better. I welcome you to the transformative journey of unlocking the true potential within you through the power of focus. Focusing is a powerful tool that can work wonders when used properly and aimed in the right direction.

Throughout this chapter, you'll learn how and where to focus (and even *hyper*-focus) to get the most out of your time and experience, fulfilling the purpose of achieving your goals.

THE POWER OF FOCUS, DISCIPLINE, AND DETERMINATION

Bruce Lee was a legendary martial artist, actor, and philosopher born in November 1940, whose legacy lives on in showcasing the power of focus, discipline, and determination to achieve extraordinary feats. Despite his early death at age 32, his profound wisdom continues to inspire generations of individuals around the world. Lee's view on the power of focus was as follows: 'The successful warrior is the average man, with laser-like focus.'

You can focus all of your energy on a very bad experience you had. It will give you the same pain—if not *more* intense pain—each and every time you think about it. The mind keeps on repeating it for you with more vivid colors, sounds, and odors, so that you feel the pain again and again. You might even start to enjoy the sight, the torture, the hurt, the grudge, until you feel the agony and fall into an irritated mood for no reason other than the mind playing tricks on you!

What's the solution? It's in your hands. You can stop all this mess in your life and decide now to start turning it around. This is exactly what you'll learn in this chapter.

What is focus?

Focus is your capacity to give your attention consciously and concentrate on anything you want. It can be a goal or a dream. It can be something good or bad, something useful that will serve your purpose, or something useless that can destroy you. When focusing, you also devote much of your energy to what you're attending to. Imagine you're directing your thinking toward something bad that's happened to you in the past. All you'll get is despair and negative emotions. Now imagine you're focusing your attention and energy on your dreams; you gain hope, motivation, and an overall good feeling in return. We want to get you into this state of feeling good, having hope, and looking forward!

Four reasons why people fall into the loop of unhappiness:

1. They don't know what they want out of life and keep distracting themselves with irrelevant exterior stimuli.
2. Instead of looking at the positives, they focus on pain.
3. They fail to console, alleviate, and reassure themselves. They simply don't know how to make themselves feel good. They revert to any outward distraction to help them deal with the present.

4. They don't know how to turn their focus to their own minds and the things that matter.

From here, the importance of focus establishes itself as a powerful tool to achieve goals and as a means to conquer misery and bring happiness and tranquility into our life.

Still not sure? Here's the story of Emily—a common tale of an everyday hero.

Allegory of the power of focus

As our story begins, Emily was an unhappy young girl lost in her dreams. She had big ambitions of leading a successful life according to her age and aspirations. She wanted to get good grades at school and be able to enter a reputable university of engineering. Yet she found herself constantly distracted and scattered, unable to progress toward her goals. One day, Emily met an old, wise mentor who guided her through the importance of focus. Inspired by the concept, Emily decided to direct all her attention and energy to the result she was looking for. She set clear, concrete goals for herself, avoiding distractions and negative influences. With unwavering determination and laser-like focus, Emily worked diligently toward her goals each day, always keeping the end result in mind.

As time passed by, she noticed a significant change in her life. She began to make progress toward her goals. Besides her devotion to study, she'd acquired many useful habits in her daily life: She enrolled in her favorite sport, which happened to be basketball, and she registered in a chess-training academy as it taught a variety of life skills, including visualization, critical thinking, problem-solving, and many other techniques and strategies. Moreover, it helped build character. Little by little, she began to feel a sense of fulfillment and achievement she'd never felt before. She started getting better grades at school, especially in math. By harnessing the power of focus, Emily could conquer her sadness, overcome obstacles, and move confidently toward realizing her dreams.

Now that we've delved into the inspiring story of Emily, I'd like to accentuate the tactics and philosophy behind sports-specific group games. Basketball is a genuine illustration of the power of focus. Like any other team sport, it requires a laser-like focus on the end result. While playing basketball, you need to focus on where you want to go, not what you're concerned about. In other words, focusing on the solution, not the problem, is always the best road to progress. If you focus on where you want to be, your actions will move you in the direction of your focus—the right way. While focusing on your goal, you must be aware of the surroundings and anticipate the near future too. Rule #1 is to concentrate on the solution that will benefit you in any case. Dwelling on the *problem* won't be of any help. Rule #2 is to never allow your focus to deviate from your goal.

Emily imagined her life as if she were always in the middle of a basketball match. No matter what, she had to keep an eye on the end goal. She needed to keep track of the future while being totally present in the playground.

The moral of the story is as follows: When you focus on what truly matters and eliminate disturbances and toxic surroundings, you can transform your life and reach territories you never thought possible.

Mastering the art of focus

The pattern is easy, and so is changing your mood and state. If you want to feel sad, think enough about something terrible that's happened to you in the past. Picture it, animate it in your mind, and you'll begin to feel the pain. The sequence continues, and you can feel the wound hundreds of times. You can decide to stop this pattern, but only *you* can end the pain. It doesn't feel good, does it? No? Then why revert to that sad old story that only exists in your head? Equally, some people keep focusing on something they're missing, so they keep the torture going.

Better yet, focus on something good that will make you feel good. Can you remember when you were happy, accomplished, and proud? Can you relive that moment, picturing it with vivid colors and sounds? You can focus on something good that's about to happen in the future and feel high levels of excitement about it.

For us to feel good and accomplish our mission, we need to focus on the desired result. To do so, we should first:

1. Eliminate distractions and background noises.
2. Direct our sight to where we want to go, not what we fear.
3. Train ourselves to focus (and even *hyper*-focus) on the goal, until giving our full attention becomes our habit (see Figure 7.1).

The 3-step equation for focusing

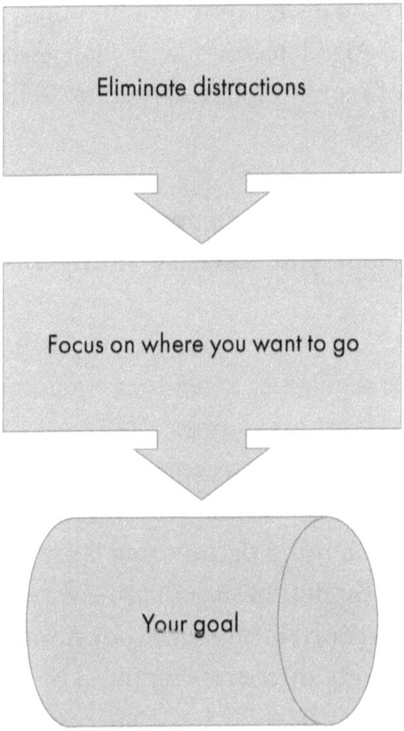

Eliminate distractions

Focus on where you want to go

Your goal

FIGURE 7.1: THE POWER OF FOCUS.

I've summed up some of the frequently asked questions around the topic of focus:

Q1: **I always revert to bad experiences I had and direct my attention to them.**

A1: As we always say, it's better to focus on the present moment, not the lost past or the unknown future. Live in the now as much as you can, enjoying every moment without the need to look back with regret, or forward with worry. This is a proven philosophy for happiness. A double-edged technique, it harnesses the stressful feelings of regret about the past, as well as the worries about the future.

Q2: **It's often not easy to maintain sight of the end result when you have so many distractions on the way.**

A2: Using the sequential three-step equation for focus will help keep your eyes on the end result while eliminating distractions. However, we must first eliminate all distractions, whether internal or external. For internal interferences, mind decluttering is a great technique to start with. By eliminating all unnecessary thoughts, you begin progressively clearing your mind, thus sharpening its powers of concentration. The same applies to external disturbances. It's even easier to remove any outside upheaval by stopping unwanted newsfeeds, silencing your phone for a while, ejecting negative or toxic people from your life, getting rid of any bad habits that won't serve your goals, and instilling good habits into your daily morning routines.

Focusing on where we want to go, not on what we fear—in other words, focusing on the solution rather than the problem—will bring many benefits.

Q3: I'm always looking at what I fear most, which is hindering me.

A3: Being optimistic is the key to solving any problem. It infuses hope and positive thoughts, decreasing the power antagonistic ideas may have over you. Again, focusing on the problem won't help, but focusing on solutions will! At the very least, it will change your perspective toward hope and positivity. From the law of attraction, we learned that being happy is a positive attribute; expecting good, then, is a strong tool to attract more of it. When you think positive thoughts, you attract more positives to your life. The same happens when you think bad thoughts. Don't look at what you fear most, as this hinders you. Instead, change your sight—look at what you love most, which will motivate you and trigger the best in you.

In conclusion, whatever you direct your attention to becomes your reality. So, focus well!

Actions for readers

Here are my calls to action, derived from this chapter:

1. Don't waste your time and energy on unnecessary tasks; focus on the important ones instead.
2. Don't fall victim to internal distractions before eliminating external ones. Doing the latter will clear your mind, leaving the necessary space to focus on the task.
3. Invest a stronger sense of purpose in every job you do. Working with clear intentions in mind makes it easier to direct your attention and reap more enjoyable and fulfilling experiences.
4. Becoming mindful of what's happening in our minds is interesting yet fruitful. We can identify some negative self-talk and discard it altogether, or we can catch our minds wandering. Studies have shown that the mind can wander anywhere from 30 to 50 percent of our waking hours. Once you notice this happening, you can get back on track faster.
5. In whatever you do, focus on the present instead of dwelling on the past or anticipating the future.

WHAT'S NEXT?

Since we've reached Step 5 of the Ultimate Happiness Formula, the next step is to *embrace pain*. While nobody can stay permanently happy, it's equally true that nobody can remain sad permanently. There's a wisdom behind any cycle in life. Being depressed can sometimes prepare you to receive more light in your life. Meanwhile, being happy can be interrupted by bad times, and nothing is guaranteed in a world of surprises. There's always a threshold, or a minimum level of unhappiness, each of us can reach. Some interesting findings, provided by auxiliary research on happiness, suggest that in the long run, very bad events and very good ones do not seem to have a noteworthy effect on the overall happiness of any particular person. The reason behind that finding is that most people tend to revert to some kind of threshold of happiness. Within a timeframe of two years, it is anticipated that any person will return back to resume life as usual, at the same baseline of happiness. This is even applicable to the most devastating life events, as per the groundbreaking study titled 'Lottery Winners and Accident Victims: Is Happiness Relative?', conducted by Phillip Brickman, Dan Coates, and Ronnie Janoff-Bulman in 1978. They found that lottery winners and individuals who had severe accidents both returned to their baseline of happiness after approximately one year. This finding confirms once again that individuals have a psychological set point for happiness that remains relatively stable despite external circumstances.

As humans, we seek one pleasure after another because the surge of happiness left after a positive event will likely return to a steady baseline over time, a concept known as the Hedonic Treadmill.

Throughout the next chapter, we'll discuss the power of pain and the influence it can have in reaching a stable, consistent, and sustainable level of happiness.

Don't resent moments of pain; just embrace them and flow with them. Later, you'll understand the sequence.

YOUR SPACE

Chapter 8

| FIND YOUR PURPOSE |

| TUNE IN TO THE 'TRUE YOU' |

| UNDERSTAND YOUR EMOTIONAL STATE |

| ACCEPT THE POWER OF QUESTIONS AND WORDS |

| UTILIZE THE POWER OF FOCUS |

| EMBRACE PAIN | ⬅ *We are here*

| TAKE ACTION |

CHAPTER 8
BEYOND PAIN

Embrace Pain and Reach New Heights

I know you've longed to hear these words for so long, and yes, I'm here to tell you that *your pain is valid!* You have every right to feel the ache, the hurt, and the wounds. But listen to me: Your pain is here to serve you for a reason. Please don't underestimate the power it carries. Accept it, acknowledge its presence, and take advantage of it.

To simplify, pain forces you to change, giving you the ability to choose and the right to start all over again. This is the real power—can't you see?

This chapter is tailored to challenge your old assumptions and belief systems, stretch your imagination, and reach new heights and horizons. It's designed to make you realize the limitless options and endless possibilities there for you. It will open your eyes and soul to a new world and a new mode of thinking. Are you ready?

'The world is changing, why don't we change? The mode of work is changing, why don't we adapt?' This is Timothy Ferris, in his book *The 4-Hour Work Week: Escape the 9–5, Live Anywhere and Join the New Rich*. Ferris is an American entrepreneur, investor, and podcaster; his book, which has been a *New York Times* bestseller, focuses accurately on the current workplace, the consequences of sudden job loss, and its impact on financial instability, emotional distress, and even loss of identity and purpose.

Ferris explains:

> *I have quit three jobs and been fired from most of the rest. Getting fired, despite sometimes coming as a surprise and leaving you scrambling to recover, is often a godsend: Someone else makes the decision for you, and it is impossible to sit in the wrong job for the rest of your life. Most people aren't lucky enough to get fired and die a slow spiritual death over 30–40 years of tolerating the mediocre.*

I hope by now the statement has been made clear. Since we know that we live in an unprecedently unusual world, we have to change the rules of the game. Do you agree with me?

WHY EMBRACE PAIN?

What we considered before as extreme is now the norm—or perhaps the new norm. Although I strongly advocate happiness as a way of living, I now suggest embracing the art of letting bad things happen, as sometimes there's no escape. It can be better to accept the pain and move on until the wave passes. I believe that pain is self-limiting and has its own way of vanishing, just like the way it started—*all of a sudden!*

Think about a moment in your life when a sad event took you by surprise: the loss of a loved one, a severe sickness, or the loss of a job. Any of these would place you in deep depression. There's nothing you can do. The only way out is to surrender to the cycle of pain until it goes away little by little, all by itself. No matter how long it takes, it will pass by—and by the time it does, you probably won't be the same person anymore. Before the wound heals, the lesson becomes well-learned, and the person becomes grown enough to move on with their life.

A case study

I received this letter from F. S. Farida, who was impacted by the great downsizing and business closures in 2020 due to the pandemic. I received Farida's permission to print her letter as-is in my book.

Dear Hoda,

I wrote this letter especially for you, to explain how I am feeling right now, today and after all I have been through. As you worked closely with me you know exactly the shock I took, when I was given notice to leave the job I loved and spent more than eight years performing at my best. Today, October 23, 2023. I am writing you to inform you, that I am in the same job, with the same company, in the same capacity. I received a promotion with an increase in salary last year. I believe my story is of value, and what was done from my side during 2020-2021 is worth narrating. Moreover, I believe, my anecdote might benefit many people who may be facing similar circumstances at workplace.

In September 2020, my boss in a phone call decided to terminate my work permanently. Without getting into more details of the pain I went through or the wound it left me with. It took me ten critical days, to get back on my feet again, connect to the upper management and ask for a remote working trial- period, of three months only- on a commission basis.

Over these three months, I demonstrated the following:

1. Elimination all time-wasters, like unnecessary office meetings, social interruptions, driving to the office, saved 30 percent of my time. Thus, gave me more time to hyper-focus on the most important tasks to be done.
2. An increase in quantifiable productivity.
3. A Lowering cost for the office.
4. An Increase in work automation, thus an increased speed in delivering the required tasks.
5. A happier and more creative employee with the least supervision.

Before completing the three months trial, I was back at work as a full time employee, on a Thursday remote-working basis and backed with some additional benefits. I set the example, and proved my worth on a performance-base and not on an office-presence base. Nevertheless, I showed case myself to be too expensive for them to quit!

Thank you Hoda for your guidance, support and believe in me. Your time was highly efficient and appreciated.

F. S.

As reflected in her message, Farida offers a great example of a strong personality who turned circumstances upside-down in her favor. She gained much confidence and trust in herself after this crisis. She discovered her net worth and grew up to be an enlightened and brilliant woman.

You can write down your painful experience on the blank page at the end of this chapter. Don't underestimate your story, as it might inspire someone else to overcome their agony and turn the situation upside-down. If you want it published, email me at hsobkyl@yahoo.com (with the subject *Pain Experience*).

A profound look beyond pain

Even pain has its role, paving the way for serious transformation in our lives. I urge you not to underestimate its power. Through it, significant and lasting improvements take place. This so-called *momentum of transformations* is nothing short of extraordinary. In this unique opportunity that occurs rarely, it's considered lucky to grasp and embrace the challenge and reach a point where life is never the same again. As the saying goes, *opportunities are fleeting and may present themselves only once.* It's up to us to seize these moments and make the most of them. Otherwise, we risk being haunted by perpetual regrets and unfulfilled aspirations.

To keep the story brief, being faced—even once in a lifetime—with great hardship, sorrow, or calamity is sometimes good. It can be the only irrefutable trigger behind any meaningful change that lasts forever.

WHEN CAN INITIATING A MAJOR CHANGE IN YOUR LIFE BECOME COMPULSIVE?

True progress can occur when the pain of staying the same outweighs the pain of change. Change becomes not a possibility but a necessity at this critical juncture, like an arrow hitting its mark (see Figure 8.1).

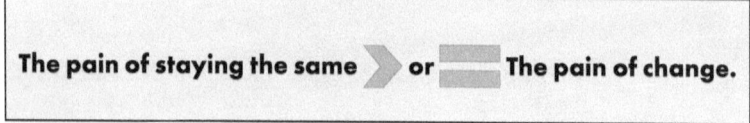

FIGURE 8.1: WHEN DOES INITIATING CHANGE BECOME A NECESSITY?

I'm not here to chase change for the sake of change, as mentioned before, but I *am* here to embrace pain as a catalyst to improve the quality of my life. Rather than seeking fleeting happiness, I aim to cultivate lifelong wellbeing, leading to *sustainable happiness in an ever-changing world*.

This philosophy forms the core of the flow of thoughts in my book, *Sustainable Happiness in an Unsustainable World*.

The philosophy behind allowing bad things to happen

Embracing pain and allowing bad things to happen is a unique method of moving forward. But to apply it, it's important to do the following:

1. Acknowledge and accept that you're in a low period that will pass by.
2. Don't resist your own passivity, weakness, and fatigue. Exhaustion is a natural part of your recovery.
3. Don't underestimate your own feelings and emotions. Instead, attend to and listen to them—they're here to guide you through making the right changes.
4. Avoid complaining; instead, learn that regret won't help.
5. Avoid reactively taking abrupt or bold decisions, which could be a fatal mistake.
6. Ignore disruptions and learn to say *no*.

Even if you do nothing, this phase will pass by and eventually lead to a better path. Trust me: Miracles that will transfer you to a better-suited place *do* happen. Life is good, but we must learn to flow with each cycle.

It's not for everyone!

Eight signs that indicate you're close to a significant life transformation, and how to embrace it.

As you grow, you start to notice a shift in your priorities. Things that used to interest you lose their spark, and goals that used to motivate you suddenly lose their drive. How you spend your time with others, your social life, and the places you used to go may not bring the same joy as they used to. Even going to work may no longer bring you the same outcome as it did before. We all fall into certain patterns in our lives, but when the old prototype is no longer working and we're most confused, the radical change we're seeking is closest. These are tangible modifications: Who you are is about to change and grow, and that transformation is coming. A quantum leap is taking place. It's worth learning that when your life is about to disintegrate, the things that are falling apart are exactly the things that won't serve you in the coming phase—the next evolution of the person you're becoming.

This transformational phase can be painful and scary; remember, though, that growth is impossible without vital change. We all have that longing for the status quo. We want things to remain the same forever, so we don't lose the patterns keeping us safe and within our comfort zone. We're so afraid to lose our ability to predict what will happen next. However, a transformational journey is exactly the opposite. Stress, anxiety, and confusion are all associated with the phase of transformation. Even negative emotions can be an indicator of positive change. The question now is:

How do you embrace the change?

1. The best course of action is to surrender to the process and let go of the things that no longer benefit you.
2. Calm down and relax your mind. Not everything that's happening is understandable right away. Just trust the process.
3. Remember that change is always a threat; there's no quantum leap or transformation without change.
4. Acknowledge that your old patterns aren't working anymore.
5. Be certain that change is the only constant truth in life. All you can do is move on and flow with it.
6. Sometimes, you must withdraw from habitual activities and spend more time alone. This allows you to stay closer to your true self and focus on your needs. Don't hesitate to do so, as it's needed for the evolutionary phase to take place.
7. As changing takes enormous energy, you may have many new thoughts that disrupt your sleep. During this part, just listen to your body.
8. Finally, old relationships may change or fade away. That part can be painful, but this is a journey of spiritual growth. Some people will grow along with you, while others may not be ready for (or won't understand) the positive change you're going through. It's hard—but nevertheless, you have to let go.

Bonus Material

Here's a bonus link to the episode 'The 8 Signs Your Life is About to Change', which explains how you know you're at a major crossroads in your life. You can scan the QR code above or go to my profile (elsobkyhoda) on Instagram, searching for the episode with the title above.

I receive many questions about the various work modes in today's turbulent world. I've summed up the three most relevant questions in the following section:

Q1: **I've been working a 9–5 job with a good, stable income stream to cover my obligations all my life. Since the pandemic, I've been haunted by the idea of starting a business on my own, based on my passion, to secure a consistent income in these turbulent post-pandemic work conditions. Now, the question is: employee or entrepreneur?**

A1: First let's define the new entrepreneurial world, then we can eliminate what it's not. I call this NEBP, or the New Entrepreneurial Business by Passion. This is a new business based on a person's true passion, where someone pursues what they really enjoy, then finds the right tools to monetize it. It's not always a family business, a solid product, or a service-based business; nor does it have to be a guaranteed income-generator or an experience-builder for a fresh graduate. I believe the NEBP is a good option for seniors and older generations, as it has all the factors that enhance freedom: what you do, where you do it, when you do it, and with whom you do it. It offers all the flexibility in the world, equipped with today's advanced technology for remote work. Today, the percentage of successful entrepreneurs compared to those who have failed varies. But generally, the success rate is far lower than the failure rate: A quick online search can easily reveal statistics that show failure rates of between 80 to 95 percent. According to Josh Howarth, in his 2023 article on explodingtopics.com (which is widely used by companies to explore trends before they happen), up to 90% of startups fail.

So, don't take that risk unless you're forced to, or unless you can afford many setbacks and failures until your business has the chance to become solid.

Q2: **I'm a new retiree, starting to find out what I can do with my time. Interacting with people at the office was my social time, so what's the best way to use my time outside the office now?**

A2: First of all, let me explain the concept of 'doing less is doing more' in the sense that doing less (i.e. less work) is, in fact, doing more things of greater personal value. It's not about being lazy (or busy doing nothing); instead, it's about being more productive. Remember that the freedom to choose is true power. When you've eliminated office distractions, you've now regained more than 30 percent of your time to focus on other matters that are more important to you, such as what you love to do, what you should do, and what you can do. Fewer distractions mean less stress, better sleep quality, more freedom and time to exercise, more regular medical check-ups, more quality time with loved ones, and more time to pursue your passions. Take time to adapt and design your new lifestyle. Mind decluttering is a good way to clear your mind from unnecessary thoughts, giving you space to welcome new ideas. You can even jettison toxic friendships and allow yourself to welcome new social circles and new hobbies, for example. Remember that life is *only* efficient and *more enjoyable* when you work at your own pace, during the times when you're most effective!

Q3: During the pandemic, I followed all your episodes on happiness, and now I have a direct but empathetic question, which is: 'Is there really a "dream job"?'

A3: To answer this difficult question, let's define the term 'dream job'. In today's terminology, a dream job gives you the freedom to choose, which is the real power! Imagine owning your time fully, having the power to choose. Another criterion would be the job that can take less time and offer the most revenue. Imagine more leisure time *and* more passive earnings. Before the pandemic, such a matrix wouldn't have been realistic, but today, through remote work and automation, it's tangible. By eliminating all possible distractions accompanying any job description and liberating the need for a particular location, a dream job is accessible. It's estimated that Generation Z (aged 12–33 today) is more inclined toward entrepreneurial jobs. Some of them have already successfully established profitable businesses.

Actions for readers

1. Since pain is irrefutable in life, accept it and flow with it. You'll understand the lesson later.
2. Life consists of cycles; some are good, and others are bad. Respect the sequence and learn from it. In the end, all will pass.

3. From the above, we can learn that there's an art to allowing bad things to happen. Sometimes, it can lead to valuable lessons and personal growth, demonstrating the wisdom of accepting and learning from such experiences.

WHAT'S NEXT?

All the above strategies, steps, and sub-steps are productive when used. Essentially, *nothing really works unless you do!* This is the main objective of the next section, so allow me to stop here and remind you *to do the work you know you should do.* By now, you can probably guess what the next chapter is about: taking the right action, building and strengthening commitment, and building stamina for persistence, grit, and endurance. Of all the personal traits I know of, persistence outweighs even ingenuity in accomplishing goals and receiving good fortune. Consistent effort is a determining factor between two persons in otherwise similar circumstances: One will be genuinely successful, while the other won't. In Benjamin Franklin's words, 'Well done is better than well said.'

YOUR SPACE

Chapter 9

- FIND YOUR PURPOSE
- TUNE IN TO THE 'TRUE YOU'
- UNDERSTAND YOUR EMOTIONAL STATE
- ACCEPT THE POWER OF QUESTIONS AND WORDS
- UTILIZE THE POWER OF FOCUS
- EMBRACE PAIN
- TAKE ACTION ← *We are here*

CHAPTER 9
DO THE WORK!

Nothing Will Change Unless You Do

In his book *Do The Work*, Gary J. Bishop refers to starting the journey of change in our lives. He says, 'You are not defined by what's inside your head. You are what you do. **Your actions.**' From here, I've decided to start my journey and this chapter of my book. No matter what you say, or how and why you say it, what matters in the end is what you do, how you do it, and why you do it! What you actually do is what defines you. *Action is king!*

Indeed, a long internal process always takes place before the action is taken. But once the action is taken, it defines and identifies you.

There's an internal process that occurs before we act. If we view it from the inside out, we find that we have core beliefs that formulate our values. These stem from our attitudes, forming thoughts and feelings.

Finally, we reach a stage where we choose how to behave and take action. We make choices based on what we think and how we feel. Then, our choices lead to our decisions, in turn leading to our actions!

DO WHAT YOU KNOW YOU SHOULD

As you see, an ongoing filtration system within you influences the decisions you make and the actions you take throughout your daily life. Whether it's a crucial decision or a trivial, non-impactful one, it all goes through our filtration system. There's a science behind any desired behavioral change. This chapter will offer a deeper understanding of your inner operating system, equipping you with the tools to make better decisions and take sound actions that elevate your quality of life.

You have a choice: Stop accepting your unattained desires, stand up for your happiness, and pursue significance in your life. This chapter will inspire you to do what you know you should!

EXPERIENCE IS THE BEST TEACHER

How many times have you been deceived by your inaction? Do you desire something out of your comfort zone, but simply lack the ability to fulfill it? How often have you seen the spark in your eyes caused by others' success, yet felt unable to endure it? How many times have you felt incompetent, inefficient, and insufficient? How many times have you felt weak, powerless, and unfit? The truth is that we all have moments of weakness, fragility, and vulnerability. But this isn't the end—making this your starting point is in your hands.

Through actions (which include failures deriving from trial and error), experience develops. Involvement, practice, and familiarity with any situation increase your likelihood of success. Taking action sharpens your wits and supports your efforts in the trials that follow. It's a prerequisite to embrace failure as a stepping stone to success. Each setback offers an opportunity to learn, adapt, and improve. Learning from failure while refining our actions is the right approach.

The knowledge, involvement, and practice you get from the action you take are worth millions. They all contribute to forming your know-how base, so consider it a training foundation that elevates your maturity, wisdom, understanding, patience, grit, and exposure. All of these shape your experiences, which are the best educator.

My grandma always told me, 'Don't go around befriending maleficent, toxic people.' In my young mind, I thought this was old-fashioned until one day, my dad told her, 'She's a stubborn little girl. Let her try.' So they let me try, which allowed bad things to happen. The experience was tough for my age. But I must admit, it was the best teacher, and since then, I've learned my lesson well—you know what I mean! I profoundly understand what it means to be surrounded by loving and kind people. Since then, I've embraced kindness as a lifestyle, and it will always remain one of my greatest values in life.

Did you get my point about *letting experience teach you?*

ACTION IS KING

Taking action, even if it seems unsuccessful, adds to your knowledge and understanding. It provides you with the necessary data to take action again, but more importantly, to avoid repeating past mistakes. With each trial, you're also changing the sub-steps required to approach your final goal. To refine your actions, you need to revise five elements:

1. Your beliefs.
2. Your values.
3. Your thoughts.
4. Your attitude.
5. Your choices.

By 'choices', I mean the new decisions you make based on your overall experience, beliefs, values, thoughts, and attitude. Making better choices means improving by replacing old habits and behaviors with more efficient and fruitful ones. Every choice we make carries a trade-off or consequence for which we should be held accountable. A conscious choice allows us to create something new or begin a fresh trajectory.

We can live in perfect harmony and stability when balancing these five elements. Our behavior becomes a natural result of our accordance with our veritable selves, and our decisions and actions yield fruit. Making the right choice and taking action at the right time is the basis for a breakthrough.

What is a breakthrough?

It might seem like a breakthrough is an overnight product. But in reality, it might take years and years to adjust your inward processes and reach the pinnacle of readiness when opportunity knocks at your door.

Bonus Material

Looking for more inspiration on the topic of breakthrough? Scan the QR code above, or go to my Instagram page (elsobkyhoda) and click on the best-voted topic for 2021. To find out more about happiness and many fulfilling topics, don't forget to subscribe to get the latest episodes.

Hank Fieger, a professional observer of human behavior and the author of *Behavior Change*, offers a view from the inside out about how our internal operating system works (see Figure 9.1, produced for the purpose of this book).

OUR INTERNAL OPERATING SYSTEM

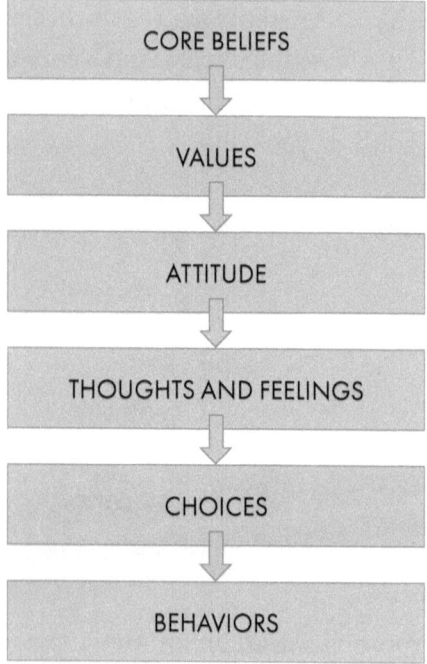

FIGURE 9.1: HOW WE SHAPE OUR OWN REALITY.

Let's begin with a wise aphorism: 'Actions speak louder than words.' Action is crucial; to understand its importance, we must find out where it originates. As explained by the above diagram, behavior stems from many elements:

1. Our core beliefs: What is our ideology, our mentality, our mindset, and our spirit?
2. Our values: What are our ethics in life, our standards, our conduct codes, and our ideals?

3. <u>Our attitude</u>: What are our notions in life, our viewpoints, our philosophy, and our approach to things?
4. <u>Our thoughts and feelings</u>: What is our psyche and character, and what are our emotions and sentiments?

Based on the above, we choose how we behave, as well as how our actions manifest in the concrete world. This is how things work out for us. This is our internal operating system and how we perceive things. We see them as *we* are, not as they really are!

Obviously, once more, the real work is within. I learned from several coaching sessions I attended that to change any behavior, we must first check these foundations (discussed above). Then, everything else aligns to reach that final stage of behavioral change. In other words, to change any undesired behavior of any child, husband, wife, family member, or employee, the change has to come from within to be solid and sustainable.

YOUR BELIEF SYSTEM

What are your stories about money?

Drawing on my own observations, I'd like to share two different stories about money. Each case study reflects how our core beliefs affect our perception.

The first is about a client struggling to start a private business. Each time she tried to initiate a new idea, product, or service, things wouldn't work well. First, she used professional help to study the market, refine the product, target end-users, secure finance, and all related matters. Yet even after patiently carrying out several trials, she had to close three different businesses. Each of these failures was due to her unrealistic expectations, coupled with her failure to meet market needs and approach clients.

On her fourth attempt, she approached me. After sitting with her and studying the proposed project together, I went further, studying her psyche as well as her core beliefs about money and starting a new business. Suddenly, she revealed that her father was never successful in business. Out of loyalty to him, she refused deep within herself to be successful while her father wasn't.

Once we identified this belief, we knew what the *real* work would involve: removing the belief that wasn't serving her. We needed to replace this with a more fulfilling belief, such as how her father would be proud of her if she were successful, and how happy he would be to feel his daughter has accomplished what he couldn't. Since then, things gradually improved, and money finally started to find its way to her bank account!

The second case concerns a middle-aged woman who'd never thought of working to secure positions that reflected her experience. When we looked deeply at her values and beliefs, we realized that she believed having a lot of money was bad for a woman, and that she should depend on a male figure like her father, brother, or husband as a source of income instead. She also presumed that having a consistent income stream was unsafe for lasting marriages. The guilt went on and on, based upon false and unrealistic convictions that would unquestionably keep money at bay. Believe it or not, this was the root cause that hindered her from negotiating her worth, asking for a salary increase, and excelling at work.

Money is so important, yet perplexing. For some people, money comes naturally. For others, money barely reaches them. Many studies and books discuss the thing called *money* and how it makes the world go around. How are some people lucky or smart enough to attract it, while others aren't? To answer this, I'd like to return to the root cause and examine how each individual perceives money.

Many questions might arise while reading this chapter. I've summarized the three most relevant ones below:

Q1: **I've been ready for an opportunity to knock at my door all my life, but it never did. This is how I see it: Some people are just luckier than others. Do you agree with me?**

A1: To answer this question, let's first define 'luck'. For me, luck is being prepared, skilled, and ready to act when the right moment presents itself. This means that success isn't based solely on luck, but on the readiness and capability to seize opportunities when they arise. Success occurs when a person's ready to take advantage of a situation or opportunity. So, when opportunity and readiness come together, we might say that we're lucky—or, to put it another way, we were just at the right place at the right time!

Sometimes we're prepared, yet the opportunity doesn't come. At other times, opportunity knocks at the door, but we're unprepared for it. Only when both come together can we make the most out of these favorable circumstances.

Q2: Talking about behavioral change, how effective is the above-explained internal process in achieving the required improvement in habits and performance?

A2: When we embrace our authentic identity, we can experience a transformation in our lives. The more we accept and understand ourselves, the better our chances of achieving change. The above case studies about two different people's perceptions of money are a good example of how our internal process can play tricks on us. So, the more we align, understand, and empathize with ourselves, the closer we are to improving our overall behavior—and thus our quality of life.

Q3: Since taking action is king, how about taking the wrong actions?

A3: Taking action, even if proved incorrect, is better than doing nothing. It's still a step in an individual's cumulative experiences. The more exposure we have, the better engagement, knowledge, and familiarity gained in each situation. All these add to our maturity, our capabilities to judge and our *savoir-vivre* (ability to live well). Those failures you were afraid to confront? Now you can face them, learn from them, and add steps that bring you closer to the change you want to see.

CHAPTER TAKEAWAYS

This chapter is a direct invitation to look inside and understand that any required change that would be reflected on the outside should happen inside first. For any shift to happen, you should be able to identify the root cause from where the behavior originated and what provoked it. What are the beliefs, values, and emotions behind the behavior? Once you're aware of all these motives and triggers, then you are in control of your attitudes and actions. The rules of the game are all internal, and you need to familiarize yourself with them.

In conclusion, the more you can connect to yourself and understand your internal operating system and how it functions, the better equipped you are to make improved choices and decisions.

For anything to happen, you should first adjust your internal process. That's because action is imperative for anything to happen—and nothing will work unless you act.

Actions for readers

- Start by revisiting your own internal operating system. Check your core beliefs, values, philosophy of life, notions, and viewpoints. What are your convictions and impulses? What are your sentiments? What triggers your enthusiasm, ardor, and zeal? What are your preferences? What do you choose? Your decisions are influenced by emotions, values, core beliefs, and so on.
- Once you're aware of all of these, you start to understand yourself better. You begin to live more in harmony with yourself. You know your motives, and you comprehend your feelings. You become aligned with the essence of who you are.
- At this point, you're in a better place. Once you've identified the behavior, you can explore its deep roots and understand where it's generated. You can then eliminate the belief that no longer serves you, replacing it with a better one that helps you achieve your goals. The more you're in synchronicity with your internal operating system, the easier behavioral change can be.

WHAT'S NEXT?

We've reached the top of our ladder of progress for learning how to live in harmony with ourselves and be happy and successful. But to evolve with this model of progression, there's one thing left: the final chapter.

To reach your potential, you need—paradoxically—to rest! The final chapter is about *rest*. Why is rest pivotal? Why is it central to your success, and sometimes even more important than work? If you're exhausted, you simply can't work. You need to rest and refuel.

In the next chapter, you'll learn all you need to know about rest, a recovery model, and work–rest ratios.

YOUR SPACE

CHAPTER 10
THE LAST CHAPTER

Rest, Stay in Peace, and Watch the
Magic Happen

Are you ready for the last chapter of this book? Psyched for the big shift? Prepared for *the paradox?*

To tap into your exquisite genius and creativity, reach your peak performance, and connect with your talents and resources, you solely need to rest. Here it is, to state it bluntly: The more you rest, the better your productivity, efficiency, and creativity.

There have been numerous studies conducted on the relationship between rest and productivity. One notable study published in the *Journal of Psychological Science* found that taking breaks and engaging in activities unrelated to work boosted creativity and problem-solving abilities. Additionally, research from the National Institute of Health (**NIH**) has shown that adequate rest and sleep play a crucial role in cognitive functioning, memory consolidation, and overall mental wellbeing. Moreover, the NIH has a specific body dedicated to sleep-related research called the National Heart, Lung, and Blood Institute, which provides valuable resources on sleep health. These findings challenge the traditional notion that nonstop work leads to greater productivity and suggest balancing work and rest is essential for optimal performance.

No wonder a growing number of studies focus on the human energy crisis and the impeded employee's capacity to work under severe pressure for long hours in an 'always-on' work environment. This has increased the importance of recovery activities and rest periods to preserve health and wellbeing while replenishing energy and creativity.

By the end of this chapter, you'll be able to appreciate and customize your work–rest balance according to your needs and comfort, thus increasing your overall wellbeing, performance, and quality of life. There's no contradiction between work and rest, or between winning at work and having a rich life. You can have it all: the harmony, balance, and richness of heart and soul.

THE SECRET OF CONTINUOUS YOUTH

Have you ever wondered how some people are more adept than others at staying fresh and strong over a long career? Or how they can renew their energy, sustain their strength, and flow in harmony for all their lives?

When researching and looking for answers to what I call 'the secret of youth and continuity of success', I looked at four of the most well-known figures in today's music and singing world. They were all top stars who'd begun their pathways to fame more than 30 years ago. I found three common denominators among those still at the top:

1. They surround themselves with people who are less than 21 years old. They also depend on many of these people in their work, along with older generations. To stay young forever, they need to get closer to youth and understand how they talk and think, what they like, how they feel, how they express themselves, what they wear, who their idols and role models are, and so on.
2. In their music and lyrics, they rely on simplicity. They all believe that words that come from the heart go straight to the heart. So, practicing honesty with themselves and with their fans is one of the key values they all hold and share. Obviously, no work of art is produced by any of them, unless it resonates with each of them and feels in complete alignment with their soul.
3. Their ability to put themselves in the creative zone is their secret weapon to make progress and stay at the top of their field.

    This mystical, powerful tool is nothing more than their ability to find the right work–rest balance. They all believe that to activate resourcefulness, new ideas, and inspiration, they must respect their need for downtime. For them, rest is the best means of regenerating, rejuvenating, and refreshing. Paradoxically, *rest is the best course of action!*

Believe it or not, they honor periods of pause and stillness. They observe and obey their intuition. They all believe that to shift their energy, they must pay homage to their gut feelings and listen to their body. For example, when it feels right to stay in bed all day long, they do so!

They know that to create new things, they sometimes have to refresh, reset, and even slingshot.

RESET

> One of the most important values you'll reap from this book is the emphasis on rest or reset periods!
>
> By taking rest phases, you're one step away from changing the quality of your whole life. You're preparing yourself to receive and accept the flow of life forces through you.
>
> Respecting the need for solitude and stillness compels us to focus on the essence of our desires and gain clarity; this is all so powerful! Whatever action you take, if you don't rest properly or enough, you'll struggle to experience the superior kind of life you're worthy of.

It's indeed a beautiful world, with a philosophy behind each winning day. Living up to your dreams will bring you peak creativity, energy, and happiness each morning. Real, original works are often produced in the very early mornings. If you apply the right morning routine each day, you integrate time for yourself, time for reflection, and time for much-needed quietude. You'll do wonders, achieving more than you think possible by reaching a notable level of performance.

True rest involves learning how to rest your mind, soul, heart, and body.

HUMAN INTELLIGENCE VERSUS ARTIFICIAL INTELLIGENCE

The importance of rest is immense, and rest periods are even more important than work. Rest is needed at all stages of life, no matter what. The implication that nonstop work produces more is now being questioned. It's simply non-sustainable! What about burnout, fatigue, exhaustion, passion depletion, destruction of resourcefulness, and failure of motivation?

The need for recharging, refueling, and re-energizing is, in fact, essential to preserve human intelligence.

In an era of artificial intelligence, why don't we work smarter and be more productive to materialize our goals effectively? Why don't we attain the right work–rest ratio to bring about accelerated yet sustainable productivity and reverse depletion, loss of motivation, and aging altogether?

THE STORY OF AMIN AND THE POWER OF TAKING BREAKS

Muscles grow not only during exertion but also during rest periods

Amin, now in his late fifties, was once a dedicated employee in the fast-paced corporate world. After an upheaval caused by the pandemic in the years following 2020, the relentless changes at his work demanded more of his time and energy with each passing day. As the stress mounted, Amin failed to prioritize his health, neglecting his wellbeing to meet the demands of his job.

It wasn't until he was forced to take a break due to downsizing and changes in the whole mode of work that he realized the toll his lifestyle had taken on him. From disturbed sleeping patterns to poor diet and minimal levels of movement and exercise, his changed lifestyle had a tremendous impact on his overall health and wellbeing.

At this point, Amin embarked on a journey of self-discovery and renewal. He realized that life wasn't just about work but also about enjoying the journey, taking care of yourself, and finding a balance between doing what you want, love, and need.

Starting to declutter his mind, soul, and body, Amin uncovered a new appreciation for rest periods. These moments of pause allowed him to reflect, reset, and realign his goals and priorities. By listening to his intuition, Amin boldly decided to venture into real estate and investing, leveraging his skills and knowledge to create a more fulfilling and sustainable career path.

Working at his own pace, Amin found a sense of freedom and flexibility that had been absent in his previous work.

Now in control of his mornings and daily routine, he crafted a lifestyle that complemented his newfound sense of purpose and wellbeing. With each investment yielding greater returns than he ever imagined, Amin understood the power of taking breaks and allowing himself to rest, recover, and grow stronger in mind, body, and spirit (see Figure 10.1).

Through this transformative journey, Amin embraced the notion that muscles grow both through exertion and during rest periods.

He found fulfillment in honoring his body's need for calmness. He found contentment in honoring his body's rhythm and indulging in the beauty of life's simple joys. He found his passion with a renewed sense of vitality and vigor. In conclusion, Amin emerged stronger, wiser, and more attuned to the rhythms of a life well-lived.

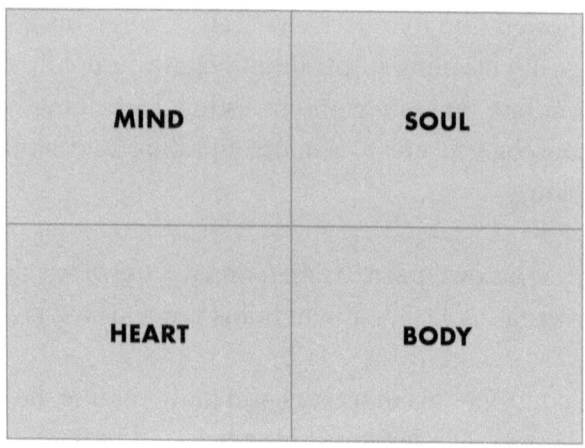

FIGURE 10.1: THE INTERNAL QUADRANT: THE WELL-LIVED LIFE COMPASS.

Success originates from within. As Stephen R. Covey, the renowned author, speaker, and expert on leadership and personal development, put it: 'Excellence and superiority are an inside job.' Covey emphasizes the importance of cultivating inner qualities such as mindset, habits, and values to achieve excellence and superiority in one's endeavors. These four life powers (illustrated in Figure 10.1)—the mind, heart, body, and soul—dwell in every person alive today. All we have to do is reclaim them. Many people spend most of their time pursuing endeavors outside themselves, but deep work and remarkable potential still reside within. In the end, it's your own life! You know better what's right for you, including what resonates better with your nature. Nurturing your internal quadrant according to your values and aspirations daily will give you a sense of liberation, adding vitality and joy to every day of your life.

THE LAST CHAPTER

WORKING ON THE FOUR INTERNAL QUADRANTS

If you move counter-clockwise through Figure 10.1, you'll find the answer to experiencing joy, happiness, and peace every day. So, let's start with the mind, then the heart, then the body, and finally the soul. Each constitutes 25 percent of the overall formula. Early morning each day, you should work on your mindset to instill positive thoughts and eliminate any negative ones that don't serve their goals. As the saying goes, *Whatever you think becomes your reality.* Your beliefs, values, and thoughts influence your attitude and behavior. Improving your mindset will improve your life.

Along with your mind, you need to clear your heart of negative emotions, such as anger, hate, frustration, envy, and jealousy. Any negative emotion you might have experienced before should be considered a learning platform, not a prison to remain in. No positive emotion will ever enter your life unless you clear out all negative ones currently residing within you, allowing positive feelings like gratitude, empathy, compassion, and kindness to flow. Doing this reinforces your mindset and gives way to positive thinking.

At this point, you've covered 50 percent of your internal quadrant. After mind and heart, we need to care for our health or physical fitness. Strengthening our body is a three-dimensional effort that relies solely on good sleep, diet, and exercise. Many scientific studies stress the elevated importance of quality sleep, eating, and exercise for vitality, longevity, and even age reversal. Adding some exercises to your daily routine, like walking, swimming, dancing, and weightlifting, can add priceless benefits to your whole existence.

We've now covered 75 percent of the well-lived life compass's four internal quadrants. To feed the mind, heart, physical, or health set, we need to listen to the soul. There are deep spiritual necessities that reside at our center of existence which can't be ignored. To elevate your soul, you need to allocate time to accessing spirituality and getting hold of the true you, which is the essence of your existence.

You need to allocate some time for silence, stillness, and even solitude. You need time to sit with your thoughts and listen to yourself. You need to calm down and slow down. You need to rest. Yes, *rest!*

We must all reclaim our spiritual authority, inner strength, and divine power. Fear, pain, insecurity, and unhappiness are all products of losing who we truly are. The soul represents the opposite of the 'I' of selfishness, imitation, comparison, and losing track of our authentic direction.

As we wrap up the book, some queries might arise for the readers. I've summed them up in the following three questions:

Q1: **Since our mind has the power to make us healthy, it can also make us sick. How can we have full control over it?**

A1: Our mind can make us healthy, but it can also make us sick—mindset is critical. Once you master your mind, you'll be happier. You'll transform the quality of your life. *It's all in the way you think!* Remember that the mind comprises 25 percent of the equation, so the remaining 75 percent is equally distributed to constitute the right balance. To have full control over your thinking and brain, you must fit in all of life's other aspects. You have to purify your heart and clear any negative emotions from it, allowing positive feelings and thinking to find their way through. Meanwhile, as a good mind needs good health, you must always take care of your physical health. Finally, your soul set encompasses your entire internal quadrant, thus leading to the healing, regenerating, and renewal process. Our souls have their own needs and requirements, which can lead to unhappiness if unmet. You can apply this every day of your life. (I'd say the sooner, the better.) If you can wake up as early as 5:00 or 6:00 a.m. every day and apply some morning routines tailored specifically for you, this will boost your performance and efficiency, thus activating your health, heart, soul, and mindset.

Q2: What basic steps can we adopt to change our state, so we can minimize waste, energy depletion, and loss of motivation while maximizing creativity, ingenuity, and talents?

A2: The basic steps to minimize energy depletion and loss of motivation while increasing productivity and creativity are easy. You create the right morning routine that fits your lifestyle and aspirations. Thus, you begin your day by setting your intentions for the day of the week based on your plans for the month and year. This way, you apply a no-waste strategy, avoiding all possible distractions. Acquiring the right habits will then come to you naturally and effortlessly. According to the Japanese *Kaizen* model, you must take small steps to reach big dreams. Don't forget to rest and take breaks along the way, which can increase your productivity and boost your creativity. This nourishes your senses and refuels you. Because muscles grow during rest and recovery periods, nonstop work won't get you any further when your energy is drained. I've taken a vacation in June, July, and August for many years. During these times, I swim, sleep, rest, walk, relax with friends and family, and play with my daughter. I simply experience life at its best. But importantly, it's during these renewal cycles that I engage in my best thinking and planning. Moreover, during this vacation, I gain my best insights. I always return to work ten times more inspired, alive, and on fire. *Time away from work isn't wasted!*

In the meantime, look at continuous learning to keep you moving forward while drawing on your enthusiasm, incentives, and eagerness to perform.

Finally, work on understanding what makes you happy—and do it. This can make all the difference, often leading to skyrocketing results.

Q3: I always had my wins at work but never fully embraced life. Consequently, I don't consider my life to be complete. Do you have an explanation for this feeling?

A3: For this, I have to tell you that you'll be old before you know it, and persistent success and victory without enjoyment is nothing. In his book *The 5am Club*, Robin Sharma said about billionaires, 'They all understood that having fun is a potent form of recovery. They all had leisure activities that recharge their empty batteries. Einstein loved to sail. Aristotle and Charles Dickens adored daily walks.' So, taking breaks, which I call rejuvenating phases or regeneration periods, creates space for new ideas to be generated. These new ideas can turn your life upside-down and even make you a fortune.

Taking rest phases, having fun, being playful sometimes, and discovering what you love to do all add to your enjoyment, creativity, and wins, thus giving your life the feeling of meaningfulness and completeness.

CHAPTER TAKEAWAYS

I'm a big fan of life. Life is beautiful. Life has always had your back. Every ending is a new beginning. Every closed door opens a realm of new possibilities. You can allow yourself to be disabled and helpless by fear and self-limitation, or you can go around and dazzle the world ... but you can't do both!

Don't abandon your dreams. Don't give up on your goals and aspirations. Instead, stay focused and committed to making them a reality. Through your dreams, you'll evolve into the person you long to be and become aligned with your true talents.

Each morning is a new beginning, a new opportunity, and a new door. Set your wellbeing and quality of life as priorities. Place high importance on your physical, mental, and emotional health, as well as pursuing experiences that bring fulfillment and happiness. Never trade them off for external validations or material gains. Life isn't meant to be about acquiring things, but about discovering life itself. Like a child, you should laugh, dance, play, explore, and enhance your capacity to generate miracles. Last but not least, *dare to be happy!*

Propositions for readers

1. Throughout life, I learned that everyone has precious gifts to offer to the world, no matter what they've been through or what they're experiencing right now. Everyone has a talent. Some are just lucky to discover it, while others aren't. The closer someone gets to their true self, the more they'll align with their soul's mission and what they can offer the world.

2. I learned that to achieve great things in life, you must be kind, empathetic, considerate, sincere, polite, patient, and honest. These seven virtues can make anyone a leader in their field.
3. I learned that whenever a door closes, a better pathway opens. Life has doorways of possibilities for everyone. We must take advantage of them by being prepared when opportunity knocks at our door. We must reach out to them. Remember, success doesn't come by chance—you have to be prepared for it.
4. I've learned that we don't regret what we've done or what we've been through (except for extreme cases of course!). People tend to regret more the opportunities not seized rather than the actions taken. We genuinely use all wrong decisions and actions as stepping stones and cumulative experiences to become better and more successful. Despite this, we only regret the chances we didn't take. To avoid mourning over missed opportunities and decisions not taken, it's important to endorse a proactive approach in life. The fear of failure can sometimes hold us back from seizing opportunities when they present themselves. But smart people learn from what they did wrong and have been through. In conclusion, we can either live forever in despair, regretting deep inside what we know we should have done; or we can live mindfully knowing that time is indeed crucial, and making the most of the present moment will eventually minimize future regrets and help us lead more fulfilling lives.

5. I learned that we shouldn't postpone our happiness until something material happens (a promotion, a new status, or money arriving in our bank account, for example). These are all simply excuses not to be happy *now*.
6. I learned that everything that's happened in your life and will occur in the future is all in your favor and for your own good. They all contribute to your personal growth and learning opportunities. Nothing happens by accident; it's all intended to respond to your needs and help you grow. It's a matter of sequence. Something bad can happen before something good; just trust the sequence. A lot of learnings arise from this process. By viewing life events as part of a sequence intended to help you grow and meet your needs, you can cultivate a positive outlook and make the most of every situation.
7. I learned that investing in yourself is the greatest gift you can offer yourself and the world. Investing in the finest books, the finest moments, the finest learning, the finest health, the finest sleep, the finest food. It will all pay off and unfold in the best ways you can imagine.
8. Finally, I learned that we reap what we sow; in other words, the outcomes we experience in life directly reflect the effort we invest, the choices we make, and the actions we take. There is a fundamental truth lying beneath, and that is our present circumstances are shaped by our past decisions and investments. Like a farmer who is expecting a bountiful harvest, so too must we invest our time, energy, and resources wisely to see positive outcomes in our endeavors. Every decision we make, every action we take, and every effort we put forth is akin to planting a

seed in the garden of our lives. Let's sow seeds of hard work, perseverance, dedication, and kindness and expect to reap a harvest of achievement, contentment, and *Sustainable Happiness*!

WHAT'S NEXT?

Now that we've gone through this journey together, I hope I've provided you with a structured framework that will enable you to embrace sustainability in your quest for happiness. Let your learnings bring about action. Whatever you decide, you can always return to the 7-Step Ultimate Happiness Formula. You can have comprehensible and explicit answers for the rest of your life while continuing to widen your knowledge and learning horizons. This would be one of the best investments you could honor yourself with. The ripple effect grows exponentially.

Finally, remember that a life of power and prosperity without enjoyment is a failure. Success and triumph, without soul, are obsolete.

Lots of love,
Hoda Elsobky (H. S.)

YOUR SPACE

SUGGESTIONS FOR FURTHER READING

The author of *Sustainable Happiness* was greatly inspired by:

Angel, B. (2018). *Unstoppable: A 90-day plan to biohack your mind and body for success.* Entrepreneur Media.

Csikszentmihalyi, M. (2008). *Flow: The psychology of optimal experience.* Harper Perennial Modern Classics.

Ferris, T. (2011). *The 4-hour work week: Escape 9–5, live anywhere, and join the new rich.* Random House.

Robbins, A. (2001). *Awaken the giant within: Take immediate control of your mental, emotional, physical and financial destiny.* Pocket Book.

Sharma, R. (2018). *The 5AM club: Own your morning, elevate your life.* HarperCollins.

Jung, C.G. (1981). The archetypes and the collective unconscious. In G. Adler et al. (Eds.) and R. F. C. Hull (Trans.), *The Collected Works of C. G. Jung,* (Vol. 9 Part 1). Princeton University Press.

REFERENCES

Chapter 1. *The Pursuit of Happiness*
1. Robin Williams. (2024, September 20). In *Wikipedia*. https://en.wikipedia.org/wiki/Robin_Williams?wprov=sfti1

Chapter 2. *A Journey Toward Redefining Happiness*
1. Alimujiang, A. (2019). Association between life purpose and mortality among US adults older than 50 years. *Jama Network Open*, https://jamanetwork.com/journals/jamanetworkopen/fullarticle/2734064
2. Urmila Rao (2020, January 29). Meditate with Urmila: Finding your purpose, *Gulf News (Tabloid edition)*, https://gulfnews.com/lifestyle/health-fitness/meditate-with-urmila-finding-your-purpose-1.69322277
3. Markus, H. & Nuris, P. (1986). Possible selves. *American Psychologist*, *41*(9), 954–69. https://web.stanford.edu/~hazelm/publications/1986_Markus%20&%20Nurius_PossibleSelves.pdf

Chapter 3. *Awaken Your True Powers*

1. Forleo, M. (2019). *Everything is Figureoutable*. Portfolio.

Chapter 4. *The* Real *You*

1. Walters, S. (1994). Algorithms and archetypes: Evolutionary Psychology and Carl Jung's theory for collective unconscious. *Journal of Social and Evolutionary Systems, 17*(3). https://www.sciencedirect.com/science/article/abs/pii/1061736194900132
2. Markus, H. & Nuris, P. (1986). Possible selves. *American Psychologist, 41*(9), 954–69. https://web.stanford.edu/~hazelm/publications/1986_Markus%20&%20Nurius_PossibleSelves.pdf
3. French, G. (2023, February 19). Connecting to yourself. *Atlas Accessories.* https://atlasaccessories.com/blogs/blog/connecting-to-yourself

Chapter 5. *The Power of Emotions*

1. Mondel, T. (n. d.). 'The 10 Action Signals: Guilt'. Thomas Mondel. https://thomasmondel.com/
2. Robbins, A. (1992). *Awaken the giant within: How to take immediate control of your mental, emotional, physical and financial destiny!* Simon & Schuster.

Chapter 6. *The Power of Questions*

1. Kabbary, A. (October 14, 2022). EDU Education Business School in collaboration with the Newcastle Business College Program, *550 Questions in Coaching.* Certificate of the Professional Doctorate in Coaching.
2. Abraham Maslow. (2024, September 20). In *Wikipedia.* https://en.wikipedia.org/wiki/Abraham_Maslow?wprov=sfti#

REFERENCES

Chapter 7. *The Power of Focus*
1. Brickman, P., Coates, D., & Janoff-Bulman, R (1978). Lottery winners and accident victims: Is happiness relative? *Journal of Personality and Social Psychology, 36*(8), 917–927.

Chapter 8. *Beyond Pain*
1. Ferris, T. (2011). *The 4-hour work week: Escape 9–5, live anywhere, and join the new rich.* Random House.
2. Frawley, R. (2024, November 17). 8 signs you're on the verge of a life transformation (and how to embrace it). *The Vessel.* https://thevessel.io/signs-youre-on-the-verge-of-a-life-transformation-and-how-to-embrace-it/
3. Howarth, J. (2023, November 4). Startup Failure Rate Statistics (2024). *Exploding Topics.* https://explodingtopics.com/blog/startup-failure-stats

Chapter 9. *Do the Work!*
1. Fieger, H. (2009). *Behavior change: A view from the inside out.* Morgan James Publishing.

ABOUT THE AUTHOR

Hoda Elsobky was born in Egypt and graduated from the American University in Cairo in 1994 with a Bachelor of Arts degree. She majored in economics with a minor in business administration, later receiving an MBA in Marketing. Hoda is a global award-winning author, keynote speaker, and happiness coach. Her greatest interest lies in the fields of philosophy and positive psychology, with a focus on self-help and wellness. Above all, she is passionate about happiness as a way of living! Certified in the science of happiness at the University of California, Berkeley, she received a professional doctorate in coaching from Newcastle Business College in 2022. Since 2005, she's been living in Vienna and then in Dubai, where she discovered her passion for writing. Outside of work, when she's not writing or reading, Hoda spends her time in charity work.

HAPPINESS IS POSSIBLE

Dare to be Happy is not just a book—it's a profound resource, designed to guide and elevate you to a superior level of fulfilment, revealing the royal path to happiness. A blend of philosophy and science that seeks to answer the question: 'What does it mean to be happy?' Written with expert guidance and real-life tips to provoke thoughts and rediscover the true sources of happiness within.

Out now.

NOTES